THE PROMISE
AND
THE PRESENCE

THE PROMISE AND THE PRESENCE

*Toward a Theology
of the Kingdom of God*

by Isaac C. Rottenberg

William B. Eerdmans Publishing Company
Grand Rapids, Michigan

Copyright © 1980 by Wm. B. Eerdmans Publishing Co.
255 Jefferson Ave., SE, Grand Rapids, MI 49503
All rights reserved
Printed in the United States of America

Library of Congress Cataloging in Publication Data

Rottenberg, Isaac C.
 The promise and the presence.

 1. Kingdom of God. I. Title.
BT94.R57   231'.7   79–22519
ISBN 0–8028–1823–4

Contents

Preface

This book began to take shape following a meeting in May, 1978, in which Emilio Castro, Executive Director of the World Council of Churches' Commission on World Mission and Evangelism, met in New York City with six persons engaged in church communications. We discussed publicity for the world mission conference to be held in Melbourne, Australia, in May, 1980, which will focus on the theme, "Your Kingdom Come."

At that time I served as Director of Communications of the Reformed Church in America. It was suggested during our meeting that I write some articles for North American church magazines dealing with the concept of "kingdom theology." During the following weeks I began to reflect on how I might approach such a project.

A month later I found myself suddenly removed from the ecclesiastical bureaucratic scene; nevertheless, I decided to spend the following months focusing on the vision of the coming kingdom. This book is the result.

The theme of the kingdom of God is once again receiving considerable attention in various theological traditions. Not only is the World Council of Churches making it a subject of special study, but a growing number of evangelical authors are emphasizing its central significance to the scriptural witness. Furthermore, a number of Roman Catholic theologians who are drawing out the implications of the kind of non-triumphalistic ecclesiology promulgated by Vatican II, are becoming increasingly kingdom-oriented in their theological approach. This book represents an attempt to enter into conversation with these various streams in Christian thought today.

I wish to mention the name of one scholar to whom no reference is made in the following pages, but who more than anyone else has influenced my thinking on the theme of this book. He is the late Dutch theologian A. A. Van Ruler, whose books and occasional personal guidance have been an inspiration to me.

Finally, a loving "thank you" to my daughter Marcia is in order. During her senior year in high school she assisted me by typing the manuscript.

I The Gospel of the Kingdom

1. THE COSMIC VISION

The biblical witness concludes with a promise and a prayer: "He who testifies to these things says, 'Surely I am coming soon.' Amen. Come, Lord Jesus!" (Rev. 22:20). In the last analysis all biblical faith finds its source in the divine Word of promise and ends in a prayer for the coming of the Lord and his kingdom.

The promise and the prayer at the end of Revelation must be read in the context of the glorious apocalyptic visions contained in John's testimony. Amidst the sound of trumpets, loud voices are heard from heaven saying, "The kingdom of the world has become the kingdom of our Lord and of his Christ, and he shall reign for ever and ever" (Rev. 11:15).

Most biblical visions of hope include the element of judgment. So also does the Apocalypse of John:

> And I saw the dead, great and small, standing before the throne, and books were opened. Also another book was opened, which is the book of life. And the dead were judged by what was written in the books, by what they had done. (Rev. 20:12)

But the final word belongs to grace and the triumph of God's redeeming power.

When John, a prisoner on the island of Patmos, heard the voice from heaven saying, "Behold, I make all things

1

new" (Rev. 21:5), it was a kind of final summation of the essential vision found throughout the Scriptures. Far from being an afterthought or a postscript at the end of the story, the idea that God the Creator is recreating the world is the central theme of the Bible.

The Bible is a futuristic book. Its authors were people drawn by a vision of God's new tomorrow. Their whole outlook and way of life were determined by what they believed about the future.

This is what theologians mean when they claim that the Bible is through and through eschatological. In the past, eschatology has usually referred to the doctrine of "the last things," meaning that it deals with such questions as the end time, the last judgment, and life after death. These topics were commonly relegated to a few brief pages at the end of theology books.

In recent decades, however, it has become increasingly recognized that our whole way of life here and now is affected by our vision of the future of the Lord. We cannot speak biblically about any aspect of our faith if we leave out the futuristic dimension. For theological reflection this means that eschatology can no longer be treated as an appendage, but must be part of our outlook on every point of doctrine.

"I am a pilgrim of the future," the great Catholic scholar Pierre Teilhard de Chardin used to say. As a paleontologist he had devoted a major part of his life to the study of the past. Although he passionately devoted himself to those studies, an overwhelming vision of God's future permeated all of his works. This is what the Bible does to people; it confronts them with the Word of promise, recreates them into a people of hope, and sends them on their way into history.

In the Scriptures Abraham is portrayed as the prototype of a person who has met the God of promise and responds in faith. In very few and simple sentences, the

Bible highlights the drama of a human pilgrimage. The Jewish scholar Martin Buber has referred to Abraham as "a nomad of faith." Abraham heard the promise, received a summons to go, and went on his way (Gen. 12:1–4).

Scriptures state repeatedly that Abraham believed God. The whole story of his life is a witness to a faith that is filled with trust, a life in which the divine promise becomes expressed in the practice of hope.

According to the book of Hebrews, Abraham journeyed in obedience without knowing exactly where he was to come out. His vision made him an adventurer. That there was a famine in the promised land when he arrived, and that he lived there all his life as a foreigner, did not dim his dream. Abraham, who always lived very close to the soil, is pictured as having *urban* dreams, looking forward to "the city which has foundations, whose builder and maker is God" (Heb. 11:8–10). In short, he dared to envision new realities beyond the scope of his immediate experiences.

The promise to Abraham refers first of all to Abraham and his descendants; they will become a great nation. But the promise does not stop there. All the generations of humanity become incorporated into the vision (Gen. 12:2–3). In the account of Noah, the rainbow became a sign of covenant between the Lord and the earth, a token of God's faithfulness to "all flesh that is upon the earth" (Gen. 9:13–17). The Lord of the universe remains faithful to his creation.

In the faith of Israel, the Exodus became the focal point of God's liberating power. This too is a story of promise that involves a summons to make a long and arduous journey to the promised land. Although the people despaired and were unfaithful at times, the God of Abraham, Isaac, and Jacob did not fail them. Through his great and mighty deeds he delivered them from bondage and led them into a new future.

The dream of a new tomorrow never died among the people of Israel, not even in the darkest moments of their history. Time and time again prophets arose in Israel to revive the vision of the future of the Lord. They too proclaimed a word of judgment and promise. The Day of the Lord would surely come, but a complacent people, trusting in their special covenant relationship with God, had to be confronted with the truth that the Day of the Lord could also become doomsday. "Woe to you who desire the Day of the Lord!" cried the prophet Amos in the midst of a corrupt and unjust society. "Why would you have the Day of the Lord? It is darkness and not light" (Amos 5:18).

The prophet pronounced his woes against those who were at ease in Zion (Amos 6:11), those who had come to take God for granted and had refused to obey his will. Yet, the promise of a new world was not forgotten:

"Behold, the days are coming," says the Lord,
"when the plowman shall overtake the reaper
and the treader of grapes him who sows the seed;
the mountains shall drip sweet wine,
and all the hills shall flow with it."

(Amos 9:13)

In the vision of Amos, God would not only restore the fortunes of his covenant people, but also encompass other nations—and indeed the world of nature—by his gracious rule (Amos 9:7,14).

The "peaceable kingdom" is beautifully described in the well-known words of the prophet Isaiah:

The wolf shall dwell with the lamb,
and the leopard shall lie down with the kid,
and the calf and the lion and the fatling together,
and a little child shall lead them.
The cow and the bear shall feed;
their young shall lie down together;
and the lion shall eat straw like the ox.
The sucking child shall play over the hole of the asp,
and the weaned child shall put his hand over the adder's
den.
They shall not hurt or destroy in all my holy mountain;

for the earth shall be full of the knowledge of the Lord as the
waters cover the earth.

(Isa. 11:6–9)

During a period of catastrophic events, when it seemed
that all attempts to reform a corrupt nation were doomed
to failure, when Jerusalem itself was captured by the Baby-
lonian armies and the people of the covenant continued to
put their trust in political intrigue, the prophet Jeremiah
dared to dream of a new covenant when the law of God
would be written on the hearts of people.

"Behold, the days are coming, says the Lord, when I will
make a new covenant with the house of Israel and the house
of Judah, not like the covenant which I made with their
fathers when I took them by the hand to bring them out of
the land of Egypt, my covenant which they broke, though I
was their husband, says the Lord. But this is the covenant
which I will make with the house of Israel after those days,
says the Lord: I will put my law within them, and I will
write it upon their hearts; and I will be their God, and they
shall be my people."

(Jer. 31:31–33)

The prophetic visions of the future of the Lord took on
a variety of forms. Ezekiel spoke about the people of Israel
in terms of a valley that was filled with dry bones. But by
the power of God death would be transformed into new life
(ch. 37:1–14). Second Isaiah, another prophet of the exile,
spoke about the Suffering Servant of the Lord (Isa. 52:13–
53:12), but also about the creation of "new heavens and a
new earth" (Isa. 65:17; 66:22).

As the Old Testament era came to a close, the prophetic visions were increasingly expressed in apocalyptic
terms. Apocalypse, with its vivid imagery and its profound
sense of historical drama, is suffused with a dualistic strain.
History is interpreted in terms of a cosmic struggle between the forces of good and evil. In the end God himself
will intervene and establish his kingdom through cataclysmic events involving the heavens and the earth. The

Book of Daniel is the most clearly apocalyptic writing in the Old Testament, as is the Book of Revelation in the New Testament.

It would be incorrect to say that the apocalyptic writings are pessimistic in their outlook. They are, indeed, full of negation as far as this present world is concerned; they pronounce an unqualified "no" against all pretentions that the kingdom of God will be established by human effort. But this is a "creative negation" (Carl Braaten), because it is inspired by a final affirmation of God's faithfulness. Thus, in actuality, they embody a deep faith that is informed by a profound hope.

Apocalyptic literature remained very much alive during the so-called intertestamentary period. Apocalyptic sects, such as the Qumran Community, separated themselves from the mainstream of Israel's life. They expected the imminent end of the present age and the inauguration of the messianic kingdom. The world was seen as so engulfed by the forces of evil and corruption, that only a direct intervention by God himself could save it.

All three synoptic gospels contain passages that are very apocalyptic (Mt. 24, Mk. 13, and Lk. 21). There are graphic portrayals of the signs of "the close of the age," including wars, persecution, and false prophets. But the vision of the future of the Lord will not be lost, because among the signs of the end time will be the preaching of the gospel of the kingdom throughout the whole world (Mt. 24:14).

After the tribulations the climactic event of history will occur, accompanied by cosmic and celestial phenomena:

> "the sun will be darkened, and the moon will not give its light, and the stars will fall from heaven, and then all the tribes of the earth will mourn, and they will see the Son of man coming on the clouds of heaven with power and great glory. . . ." (Mt. 24:29–30)

No one knows the day and the hour of the end (v. 36) but believers are admonished to be ever alert (v. 42). In "the new world" all those who have been willing to pay the cost of serving the Son of man will "inherit eternal life" (v. 29).

The views of the apostle Paul concerning the consummation of time are firmly rooted in his faith that the new age has triumphed in the cross and resurrection of Jesus Christ. Christ is the first fruit of a new humanity (I Cor. 15:15), and as Paul writes in I Corinthians 15:24, 28 (NEB):

> Then comes the end, when he delivers up the kingdom to God the Father, after abolishing every kind of domination, authority, and power . . . and when all things are thus subject to him, then the Son himself will also be made subordinate to God who made all things subject to him, and thus God will be all in all.

The biblical vision encompasses all things. The cosmic and world-historical implications of God's saving work in Christ are developed particularly in the letters to the Ephesians and Colossians. In Christ "all things hold together" (Col. 1:17)—"For in him all the fulness of God was pleased to dwell, and through him to reconcile to himself all things, whether on earth or in heaven, making peace by the blood of his cross" (vv. 19–20). Finally, it is God's plan for the fulness of time "to unite all things in him, things in heaven, and things on earth" (Eph. 1:10).

What term shall we use to express the manifold aspects of God's gracious dealings with the world as well as the unity of the biblical vision concerning God's future? The Bible itself provides us with a comprehensive term for this purpose: gospel of the kingdom. There are other ways in which the Bible describes the message of redemption that has come to us: the gospel of God, the gospel of Christ, the gospel of reconciliation, and the gospel of grace. The term "gospel of the kingdom," however, helps to remind us of the broad cosmic and world-historical dimensions of the message of redemption. It encompasses heaven and earth, the inner recesses of the human heart and the history of nations, the orders of society and the world of nature.

We must learn to speak biblically about "all things." Throughout history believers have often been tempted to focus on a *few* things, to dwell on a few favored texts or selected themes, and to build a whole theological system out of a few insights that may be valid in themselves but yet cannot carry the full weight of the gospel of the kingdom. Or, on the other hand, we have gone to the opposite extreme and have acted as though God's plan to unite all things one day means that Christians have the answers to all the questions and problems of the world.

The gospel of the kingdom opens up wide vistas, but it also keeps us focused on the heart of the matter: God-with-us—the sovereign Lord who through the initiative of his love is establishing his future in the world.

2. THE KINGDOM THEME

All three synoptic gospels stress the point that Jesus began his ministry with a proclamation about the kingdom of God. Mark reports that "after John was arrested, Jesus came into Galilee, preaching the gospel of God, and saying, 'The time is fulfilled, and the kingdom of God is at hand; repent, and believe in the gospel'" (ch. 1:14–15). Matthew, who prefers the term "kingdom of heaven" (most likely because of the practice among his people to avoid mentioning the name of God), emphasizes Jesus' teaching in the synagogues, his preaching of the gospel of the kingdom, and his healing ministry (ch. 4:17,23).

Luke, who records Jesus as saying that he "was sent for this purpose" (namely, to preach the kingdom of God, ch. 4:43) initially does not use that term, probably because his Greek readers would not readily understand the concept. Instead he tells the story of Jesus' visit to the synagogue in Nazareth where he read the famous Isaiah 61 passage about the preaching of good news to the poor, release to the captives, liberty for the oppressed, and the proclamation of "the acceptable year of the Lord." He followed this with the astounding claim: "Today this scripture has been fulfilled in your hearing" (Lk. 4:16-21). In other words, Jesus proclaimed the message of the kingdom with the clear conviction that he was standing in the tradition of the prophetic vision of the future of the Lord. His whole ministry and not just his message must be seen in that light.

Most of Jesus' hearers had some idea what he was talking about when he referred to the kingdom of God even though the term itself occurs infrequently in the Old Testament. In the Psalms, which are replete with references to God's reign, we find the actual term used only twice. Psalm 103 declares that "the Lord has established his throne in the heavens, and his kingdom rules over all" (v. 19), and Psalm 145 refers to God's kingdom as "an everlasting kingdom" (v. 13).

Yet, not only in the Psalms, but throughout the Old Testament, God's sovereign rule over the destiny of nations is confessed and proclaimed. The prophets broaden the vision of God's righteous reign to include not only the covenant people of Israel, but other nations as well (Amos 9). Later, as we have already noticed in the previous section, the vision was presented in increasingly apocalyptic language. The God of history, who led Israel out of Egypt, is the Lord of the universe who will create a new heaven and a new earth. In other words, it is not enough to confess God as the Lord of our lives; the biblical witness opens up much wider perspectives about God's saving work in the world.

As we move from the references to the kingdom in the Old Testament to the Gospel of John, there is a strong shift in emphasis from the future expectation to the present reality of the Spirit. Eternal life is here! "He who believes in the

Son *has* eternal life" (Jn. 3:36). The emphasis on the presence of the future of the Lord was certainly not missing in the synoptic gospels. The parables, which are called "parables of the kingdom," have much to say about its presence in the world and Jesus' miracles are seen as manifestations of its power: "If it is by the finger of God that I cast out demons, then the kingdom of God has come upon you" (Lk. 11:20).

The term "kingdom of God" is found only twice in the Gospel of John, both times in the story about Nicodemus and the need for rebirth if one is going to enter the kingdom of God (Jn. 3:3,5). There are those who say that in the fourth gospel mysticism totally replaces eschatology; that is, the intense future expectation of the earliest Christians is replaced by the experience of the Spirit in the here and now.

It is quite likely that John, whose gospel was written later than the synoptics, sought to address the issue of the "delayed Parousia," the fact that the imminent return of the Lord, which many among the early Christians had expected, did not take place. It was important for those believers to be reminded of the new life which is available through the Spirit in the here and now. It is an exaggeration, however, to say that John totally eliminated the perspective on the future.

Scholars who emphasize John's mysticism usually admit that there are "vestiges" of eschatology in his gospel. "The hour is coming," we read in John 5:28f., "when all who are in the tombs will hear his voice and come forth, those who have done good, to the resurrection of life, and those who have done evil, to the resurrection of judgment." Some claim that such references are later additions, others call them accommodations to the popular view of that day, while others say that they really refer to the crucifixion and John's emphasis on its elevation and glorification.[1]

A quick check in a concordance will show that in the

apostolic preaching the theme of the kingdom does not occupy the central place that it does in the synoptics. Jesus announced the coming of the kingdom; the apostolic Church proclaimed him as the Christ. However, as we shall see later, the message of Christ crucified and the message of the kingdom are closely related to each other. For the apostle Paul particularly, the new age has been inaugurated in the cross and resurrection of Jesus Christ. But the epistles also refer to those who become part of the new order of God as "heirs of the kingdom" (Jas. 2:5). In the next chapter we shall also see how the epistles contain a variety of references that describe the reality of the kingdom.

From our survey in this section we conclude that the kingdom motif constitutes a unifying theme in the Scriptures. As John Bright, in his somewhat dated but still valuable book, *The Kingdom of God*, has pointed out, the diversity within the Scriptures must not be glossed over with simplistic, unifying schemes. The Bible contains an immense diversity of literature. Differences between the Old Testament and the New Testament, as well as within these parts of the Bible itself, must be taken seriously and deserve the scholarly attention that has so often enriched our understanding of the gospel message.

Yet, according to the historic confession of the Christian community, the Bible is also the Word of God; it has a revelational unity that transcends all of its diversity. And that unity can best be described in terms of the gospel of the kingdom.[2]

Throughout the Scriptures we meet the God of Promise who confronts us with the claim of his kingdom, a God who establishes the kingdom in our midst through the power of his Spirit. Thus the future of the Lord is manifested among us. Those who participate in the new reality of the kingdom can truly be described as people "upon whom the end of the ages has come" (I Cor. 10:11).

II Dimensions of the Kingdom

1. KINGDOM LANGUAGE

"With what can we compare the kingdom of God, or what parable shall we use for it?" (Mk. 4:30). This question of our Lord comes to mind as we seek to describe the kingdom of God more concisely. As we examined a variety of visions concerning "the close of the age" in the previous chapter, it became clear that language was frequently strained to the very limits of its poetic potential. When God reveals to us through the Spirit "what no eye has seen, nor ear heard, nor the heart of man conceived" (I Cor. 2:9), we reach out for poetic imagery, parable, and symbol to describe the indescribable.

Such is also the case with the biblical witness to the kingdom. Language is such a glorious tool, and yet so limited. The kingdom of God does not "belong to this world" (Jn. 18:36 NEB), and all comparisons of the kingdom to concepts and categories of this world break down in the end. The very notion of a kingdom is problematical to many people today, and in wide circles it does not have a very positive connotation. The kingdoms which are found in the world today are not exactly what the masses of the world look forward to. Furthermore, in our day it is usually presidents and prime ministers who have more power than kings and queens. Finally, there are people who consider the term sexist and therefore wish to avoid it.

13

In view of these factors, some people prefer to talk about the *reign* of God. This is appropriate for numerous biblical passages. But the Bible also reveals something about the *context* of that reign, and then the kingdom of God must be described, not necessarily as "a place," but as a historical time and worldly space. As we shall see later, signs of the kingdom of God are established upon the earth at certain times and in certain places. The kingdom of God somehow (though in a very tentative and fragmentary way) takes shape in human structures. The word "kingdom" expresses this more adequately than the words "reign" or "kingship."

The Old Testament treats the idea of kingdom with much ambivalence, and does not always give it a positive connotation. The religious language problem is not as modern as we sometimes like to believe. People in ancient, pre-scientific cultures struggled with the language question too, although in our technological age the issue has definitely become a more urgent one.

John Calvin frequently used the term "accommodation" when speaking about God's revelation to us. God accommodates himself to our finite minds and limited thought forms in order to communicate the message of eternal salvation to us, indeed, to reveal *himself* to us. "The sublime mysteries of the kingdom of heaven," Calvin wrote, are "communicated, for the most part, in a humble and contemptible style."[1] According to Calvin, that was done not only because of our limited knowledge, but also in order to ensure that the triumph of the Word would not be attributed to the eloquence with which it was presented. No doubt he had in mind the words of II Corinthians 4:7: "We have this treasure in earthen vessels, to show that the transcendent power belongs to God and not to us."

It should also be pointed out that matters are sometimes treated as communication problems when we are really dealing with moral issues. The Bible gives us trouble not so much because of its language but because of the content of its message. We are confronted with a message that calls us to radical transformation. The gospel of the kingdom seemed as foreign to Jesus' contemporaries as it does to us because it turns our world upside down. There are "hard sayings" (Jn. 6:60) in the gospel, and there is also the hardening of human hearts (Mk. 8:17).

The above remarks lead us to the question of the use of parables in Jesus' proclamation of the kingdom. According to Georgia Harkness and others, the parables are "probably the most authentic of all the sayings ascribed to Jesus."[2] They have a down-to-earthness about them that makes them extremely appealing to that vast majority of humanity who are constantly struggling with day to day decisions and concerns. They are brief, like sermon illustrations, which makes them easy to remember. They are used to clarify issues about life in the context of the kingdom of God, and also as a form of polemics against opponents who resist the reality of the kingdom as preached and practiced by Jesus.

New Testament scholars do not agree on the question of whether parables were a commonly used teaching method among the rabbis in Jesus' day. Herman Ridderbos believes that they were.[3] But, if this is true, why do all three synoptic gospels report that the disciples inquired about the purpose of speaking in parables? In Mark 4:10, we are told, "the twelve asked him concerning the parables." Luke reports that the disciples inquired about the meaning of the parable of the sower (ch. 8:9), while Matthew specifically raises the question: "Why do you speak to them in parables?" (Mt. 13:10). Apparently, the parables are not simple and self-evident stories, as Jesus' answer to the disciples makes clear: "To you it has been given to know the secrets of the kingdom of heaven, but to them it has not been given" (v. 11). Then he adds: "Because seeing they do not see, and hearing they do not hear" (v. 13). In Luke, Jesus' reply is put even more strongly: "so that seeing they may not see, and hearing they may not hear" (ch. 8:10).

In other words, there is a key to the understanding of the parables of the kingdom; one has to know "the secret." And what is the insight that reveals the meaning of the parables of the kingdom? Why do some people see but not see and hear but not hear? The answer is that they fail to recognize that the kingdom and its power are being revealed in one who is in their midst.

For some the parables are revealing, for others they are concealing. The kingdom of God is hidden and is perceived only with the eyes of faith. Those who harden their hearts (Isa. 6:10, cited in Mk. 4:12) are not helped by the parables of the kingdom. To the contrary, they are confirmed in their blindness, and the gospel becomes a word of judgment to them. To those, however, who respond in faith, God reveals the glorious truth of his "plan for the fulness of time" (Eph. 1:10).

2. PARADOXES OF THE KINGDOM

Anyone who turns to the Bible to find a concise definition or a simple summary of the nature of the kingdom of God will be disappointed. As we survey the textual materials, we are presented with a series of statements that are often paradoxical. Yet, as we reflect on the multifarious insights provided by the biblical references to the kingdom, we gain a deeper understanding of its nature as well as its relevance for our own historical situation.

The following illustrations may help to clarify this point:

a. The kingdom of God is not *from* (the word *ek* is used in the Greek) this world (Jn. 18:36), yet it is very much related to this world. The kingdom of God does not find its source and essence in this world. Instead it enters it as a breakthrough of the power of God's future which will transform this world.

The Bible does not point us to some other world that is supposed to be far superior to the one in which we live. *This* is the world which God has created and will be saving. *This* is the world which he has loved so much that he became incarnate in it. The redemption of the world will constitute a recreation of such radical proportions that it can be called a new creation. But we should never lose sight of the fact that the kingdom of God is totally concerned with all the worldly realities that are part of our daily life experiences.

"I do not pray that thou shouldst take them out of the world," we read in the so-called high-priestly prayer, "but that thou shouldst keep them from the evil one" (Jn. 17:15). The world is the scene of the great drama of history in which the Lord of creation takes on the forces of evil. That drama is staged in the heart of every person.

Kingdom theology helps to cure us of an unworldliness that is contrary to the witness of Scripture. At the same time, it provides us with a transcendent perspective that will help us to be worldly in the right way.

b. The kingdom of God comes as a gift, but it does not come cheaply. Participation in the life of the kingdom is costly.

In Luke 12:30–33 we find these two perspectives combined in a wonderful and rich logic of faith. The kingdom is to be sought with a sense of urgency. At the same time it is a comfort to know that it is the Father's good pleasure to give the kingdom to his children. Then, without any transition at all the participants in the kingdom are called to a life of great sacrifice: "Sell your possessions and give alms . . . !

There are reasons other than economic ones which demonstrate why participation in the kingdom comes at a price. It must be received in the humble spirit of a child (Mk. 10:15), repentance is required for all who are to enter (Mk. 1:15), and the basic law of the kingdom is a life in obedient love.

The kingdom of God is a gift and a goal; we await it and we work for it. The Christian life is lived in the joyful tension of grace and responsibility, of hope and constant alertness. "According to his promise we wait for a new heaven and a new earth in which righteousness dwells. Therefore, beloved, since you wait for these, be zealous to be found by him without spot or blemish, and at peace" (II Pet. 3:13–14).

c. According to Paul, the kingdom does not consist in talk, and yet it is imperative that the kingdom be proclaimed. Jesus declared that he was sent for that purpose (Lk. 4:43), and the apostle Paul is certainly one of the last persons who would denigrate the importance of proclamation.

When Paul declared that "the kingdom of God does not consist in talk but in power" (I Cor. 4:20), he meant to contrast empty talk with the preaching of the gospel that is a power unto salvation.

The proclamation of the gospel of the kingdom is a historical force of the first order. Calvin, in his discussion of the prayer "Thy kingdom come," wrote, "This is done partly by the preaching of the Word and partly by the overt power of the Holy Spirit . . . both must be joined together in order that the kingdom of God may be established."[4]

Talk, even religious talk, can become a substitute for proclamation and thus become an obstacle to rather than an avenue for the coming of the kingdom in our midst. The same can, of course, be said of churchly pronouncements and theological writings. They can become so many words that obscure the Word.

d. "The kingdom of God does not mean food and drink but righteousness and peace and joy in the Holy Spirit" (Rom. 14:17). Yet, the kingdom can also be compared with a banquet or a wedding feast (Mt. 22:1–14).

It is important for us to remember that food and drink and all that they symbolize are not the kingdom of God. But, on the other hand, we should never forget that table fellowship and a good meal can well be true signs of the kingdom to us.

The struggle for righteousness and justice, the search for peace, and the experience of joy in the Lord must not be set over against some good fun and the little pleasures that enrich our lives. The gospel of the kingdom calls for self-denial; it also inspires the proper kind of worldly enjoyment.

e. The kingdom of God is hidden and people must not say too quickly, "Look here," or, "Look there!" (Mk. 13:21). Yet, the kingdom is discernible to those who know how to read the signs of the times. The kingdom is present as the transforming power of God's future; it is manifested in our midst through the power of the Holy Spirit. The fact that this is *God's* power is not self-evident. In that sense the kingdom does not come "with observation" (Lk. 17:20). However, those who have eyes to see will indeed see.

3. PARTICIPATION IN THE KINGDOM

The New Testament speaks about *entering* and *inheriting* the kingdom. Those two terms reflect the inner dynamics of the Bible about the presence of the kingdom in the here and now and its futurist dimension. The kingdom is offered as a present reality, but there always remains an element of promise. In the next chapter that aspect of the gospel of the kingdom will be discussed more specifically.

Repentance and rebirth are prerequisites for entering the kingdom of God, and only through a life of obedience to the divine will can it be inherited. "Do you not know that the unrighteous will not inherit the kingdom of God?" (I Cor. 6:9), writes the apostle Paul. He then lists an assortment of immoralities that preclude people from participating in the promise.

As we noticed already, one must have a humble and childlike spirit to enter the kingdom of God (Mt. 10:13-16). Those who pride themselves in their own righteousness have less of a chance of entering than sinners who face the truth about themselves (Lk. 18:9-14). The high and mighty will find it very difficult to enter the kingdom. "How hard it will be," said Jesus in the illustration of the camel and the eye of a needle, "for those who have riches to enter the kingdom of God" (Mk. 10:23-28). The disciples found this an amazing statement, and since then clever minds have been devising all sorts of ingenious schemes to explain how that camel could fulfill that difficult assignment.

Dietrich Bonhoeffer's emphasis on "the cost of discipleship" has received renewed attention in recent years especially among Christian communities where radical commitment is stressed. In his book, *Agenda for Biblical People*, Jim Wallis points out that "the great tragedy of modern evangelism is in calling many to belief but few to obedience."[5]

The story of Nicodemus, with its emphasis on the need to be "born again" in order to enter the kingdom of God (Jn. 3), is a classic example of the bafflement and embarrassment aroused by that theme, particularly in intellectual circles. Nicodemus, who was certainly among the well-educated of his day, seems at a loss for words, and when he does speak, his remark about the impossibility of reentering a mother's womb is hardly a pearl of wisdom.

On the other hand, born-again Christians have commonly shown a significant lack of interest in kingdom theology. They love to talk about conversion, but they fear that emphasizing the kingdom of God will lead them straight into what they believe to be the horrible pitfalls of the "social gospel." Thus conversion theology and kingdom theology tend to go their separate ways, which is one of the major tragedies of Christian history, because it prevents us from dealing biblically with the social implications of the gospel.

We must learn to see conversion in terms of the kingdom. When the power of God's future breaks into the present and radically renews a human heart, this is a revolutionary happening. It certainly is a central manifestation and a sign of the power of the new age. Colossians 1:13 describes it as a transfer from the kingdom of Satan to "the kingdom of the Son of his love" (ASV). There is nothing wrong with stressing the wonderful stirrings that the Spirit of God creates in the human heart—as long as it does not make us forget about his work in history.

There were periods in history when revival movements, with their strong emphasis on personal conversion, inaugurated a new era of social concern and interest in charitable causes. Conversions were seen as signs of the kingdom, when God would establish the new heaven and the new earth where righteousness would dwell. H. Richard Niebuhr has stated that Jonathan Edwards saw the surprising conversions resulting from his preaching as an indication:

> that this work of God's Spirit, so extraordinary and wonderful, is the dawning, or at least a prelude of that glorious work of God, so often foretold in Scripture, which, in the progress issue of it, shall renew the world of mankind.[6]

The New Jerusalem has begun to come down from heaven! The same theme can be found in John Wesley, who believed that God was already renewing the face of the earth, so he placed equal emphasis on conversion and social-economic justice.

A biblical kingdom theology will not be a threat to a conversion theology. Rather, it will cleanse it from the false and unbiblical kind of individualism that has so often given born-again Christians a bad name. The gospel is spread through the witness of the Christian community, and conversion that leads to a life of isolation has little to do with the gospel of the kingdom. The born-again Christian enters a community, and that community in turn is a sign of the kingdom. As such, that community is sent out to serve the world in the name of and with the vision of the coming kingdom of God. As Orlando Costas has stated so well:

> Christian conversion is a journey into the mystery of the kingdom of God, which leads from one experience to another.... Initiation in the journey of the kingdom implies a plunge into an eschatological adventure where one is confronted with ever new decisions, ever new turning points, ever new fulfillments, and ever new promises, and this will continue until the ultimate fulfillment of the kingdom.[7]

José Míguez-Bonino adds a biblical mission-dimension when he writes:

> The call to conversion is an invitation to discipleship... whether it takes the direct form of Jesus' call to follow him or the apostolic form of participation through faith in the Messianic community.... It revolves around the kingdom. Consequently, it involves a community which is engaged in an active discipleship in the world.[8]

4. THE KINGDOM AND THE POWER

As stated previously, the apostle Paul declared that the kingdom of God did not consist in talk but in power (I Cor. 4:20). The kingdom of God is the power of the new age entering our world and transforming it according to God's plan for the fulness of time.

"Thine is the kingdom, and the power, and the glory...." Thus it is now. Every time we pray the Lord's Prayer, we confess our faith in the presence of the power of the kingdom. And thus it will be according to the great vision of the apocalypse when a loud voice in heaven shall declare: "Now the salvation and the power and the kingdom of our God and the authority of his Christ have come..." (Rev. 12:10).

The power of the kingdom is the power of the sovereign Lord of the universe; it is the power of his future, the recreative power of him who has promised to make all things new (Rev. 21:5). When God reveals himself, it always means that power and glory are manifested in our midst.

We should never forget that we confess God as God, the Father, Almighty. In other words, we speak of God as one who has revealed himself supremely in the Son. Therefore, the power and the glory of the kingdom must be understood in terms of Jesus Christ, particularly in terms of his cross and resurrection. That makes a tremendous difference in how we interpret the presence of the kingdom and its implications for us today.

"We have beheld his glory" (Jn. 1:14), and we have learned that it is a glory without glamour. The glory of Christ was manifested in the barn in Bethlehem and the cross on Golgotha.

The power of the Christ is the power of the cross, which in the resurrection has been revealed as the triumph of his love. The Christian faith does not focus on "almightiness," but on the power of grace and reconciliation as they have been manifested in Jesus Christ. The power of his atoning and liberating work is now operative in history.

This all happens through the work of the Holy Spirit. As Paul expressed in his letter to the Romans, the kingdom of God means "righteousness and peace and joy in the Holy Spirit" (ch. 14:17). Rudolf Bultmann has called the Holy Spirit "the power of futurity."[9] He means that "Spirit" is the biblical symbol for the possibility of a new life or the experience that brings more authentic life. It is true that, when we find assurance of forgiveness through the Spirit, we are delivered from bondage to the past caused by guilt and are freed for the future. However, the Spirit is "the power of futurity" in a much broader sense as well. Through the Holy Spirit, the power of the new age is manifested in our midst, and when that happens, manifold signs of the kingdom are established upon the earth. Thus God's new tomorrow enters our today.

III *The Coming of the Kingdom*

1. THE GOD WHO COMES

The kingdom of God is always proclaimed as coming. John the Baptist declared that it had come near (Mt. 3:2), and Jesus also included this in his own preaching (Mt. 4:17). From its very inception the Christian Church has affirmed in faith that the power of the kingdom was being manifested among God's people. At the same time Christians have never ceased to pray for the coming of the kingdom.

This emphasis on the coming kingdom is not surprising, because we are really speaking of the activities of the coming God. He is the God of the covenant. He is the God of Abraham, Isaac, and Jacob. He is the God who keeps his covenant and always opens up new futures.

The God of the Bible hears the cries of his people and comes to liberate. "I have seen the affliction of my people who are in Egypt," says the Lord to Moses, "and have heard their cry because of their taskmasters; I know their sufferings, and I have come down to deliver them..." (Exod. 3:7–8). Moses is not sure how the people will react when he announces to them, "The God of your fathers has sent me to you." What if they wanted to know the name of the One who sent him?

The answer Moses receives to this question about the name of God is translated differently in the various versions of Scripture. The most common translation is "I AM

25

WHO I AM." Here the focus seems to be directed at the *being* of God. He is the One who *is*. Martin Buber believed that the connotation of the Hebrew was best translated, "I shall be there, as I shall be there."[1] In other words, I shall be there *in my own way*—as sovereign Lord.

In ancient religions, it was important to know the name of the deity because of the belief that once the name was known, divine power could be manipulated through magic. If Buber's translation is correct, the text would seem to point to the "otherness" of Yahweh. He is not that kind of God. Furthermore, Buber's rendering changes the focus from God's *being* to his *being there*. The God of the Bible is not known through *speculation* about his being, but through an encounter with him in history. His being is known through his presence.

"I am the Alpha and the Omega . . . who is and who was and who is to come . . ." (Rev. 1:8). The coming God is not the "Unmoved Mover" of scholastic theology: he is Immanuel, the One who comes and is present in the world in a redemptive way. The God of the Bible is always doing new things. These are the initiatives of his love. Thus he creates history, as he guides the destiny of the world to the future of his kingdom.

Biblical faith has to do with straining "forward to what lies ahead" (Phil. 3:13); it has a futuristic quality about it. "The Church's stance," according to Jacques Ellul, "can only result from a future-now-in-process. . . . It is a matter of the Lord in process of coming; that is a future which is drawing near."[2] The eschaton is coming, and *as such* it is here. We are the people "upon whom the end of the ages has come" (I Cor. 10:11).

When we say that God's future breaks through into our present, we are really talking about God himself who comes and is redemptively present in the world in order to establish the new heaven and the new earth. As a German theologian has expressed it, God's historical-eschatological dealings with the world confront us with a "presence of what is coming towards us, so to speak an arriving future."[3] Carl Braaten expresses the same idea when he uses the phrase "oncoming kingdom."[4]

Most of us have become so accustomed to think of history as evolving out of the past that we find it difficult to see the future as the formative power in the historical process. Christians are supposed to be people who have "tasted the goodness of the Word of God and the powers of the age to come" (Heb. 6:5). However, that is often not the way we come across to those around us. So much of the Church's conservatism and lack of dynamics in its life and mission is due to a loss of the vision of the future.

A kingdom theology helps us to rediscover the priority of the future and to live out the vision of the new age. The promise of the renewal of all things and the presence of the power of the kingdom through which we receive a foretaste of the future, turn life into a journey. The urgent search for God's kingdom and his righteousness (Mt. 6:33) becomes the believer's way of saying "yes" to God's future.

2. CHRIST AND THE KINGDOM

The God who comes has revealed himself supremely in Jesus Christ. "The Word became flesh and dwelt among us" (Jn. 1:14). The divine presence becomes embodied in the life and ministry of this person, Jesus of Nazareth. In him we meet the One who made his name to dwell in Israel, the One who said to Moses: "I shall be there!"

Jesus was sent to proclaim the message of the kingdom. But, more than that, in his person and ministry the kingdom of God was manifested in a new way. He, in distinction from the prophets that had preceded him, was the content of his own message. He is the King of the kingdom. The church father Origen used the word *auto-basileia* to express the truth that Jesus himself was *the*

central expression of the kingdom of God in the world. "If
it is by the Spirit of God that I cast out demons, then the
kingdom of God has come upon you" (Mt. 12:28).

The gospel of the kingdom is absolutely bound up with
the saving work of Jesus Christ. As it has been said, "He
came not so much to preach the gospel, but that there
might be a gospel to preach." The kingdom of God is rooted
in a very special way in the cross and the resurrection of
Jesus Christ. "All the promises of God find their Yes in
him" (II Cor. 1:20).

As Christians have reflected on the biblical witness
concerning the coming of the kingdom in Jesus Christ
throughout the centuries, they have placed different emphases on the significance of the various aspects of the
Church's Christological teaching: the incarnation, the
cross, the resurrection, the ascension, the outpouring of
the Spirit, and the Parousia. We shall take a brief look at
those differences in accent, because they affect the kind
of kingdom theology we affirm. It should be kept in mind,
however, that we are indeed talking about emphases. Most
Christian theologians incorporate into their thought the
various aspects of the biblical witness to Christ mentioned
above. There is a difference, however, in where they place
the emphasis, and therefore in the way they approach the
witness of the Church today.

a. Incarnation

The biblical witness to the incarnation is fundamental to a
theology of the kingdom. As we have noticed before, the
whole Bible witnesses to the coming God, and incarnation is
certainly not unknown in the Old Testament. There too we
find a constant emphasis on the presence of God in historical reality. There too we learn about redemption as it becomes embodied, very tentatively and very fragmentarily,
but nevertheless really, in historical structures.

When the New Testament testifies that "the Word
became flesh," we are confronted with the presence of the

kingdom in a new, decisive, and glorious way. The doctrine of the incarnation brings us face to face with what is sometimes referred to as the "materialism" of the Bible. We are reminded that God the Creator is ultimately concerned with earthly realities, so much so that in the Son he entered into our physical existence for the sake of the salvation of the world. The frequently quoted phrase of F. C. Oetinger is most appropriate here: "The end of the ways of God is corporeality." The biblical witness to creation, incarnation, and the resurrection of the body should caution us against false spiritualizations that can have such a strong appeal to our natural minds.

The incarnation can be viewed narrowly as well as broadly. In the former case, the so-called *assumptio carnis*, the fact that the divine Logos assumed human nature, is strongly emphasized. The Word became flesh! In the latter case, incarnation is interpreted in terms of the whole life and ministry of Jesus and particularly his atonement for sins. "God was in Christ reconciling the world to himself . . . For our sake he made him to be sin who knew no sin, so that in him we might become the righteousness of God" (II Cor. 5:19,21).

In this section we shall briefly examine the interpretations of the incarnation which focus primarily on the *assumptio carnis*, the assuming of human nature by the divine Logos. Some theologians see the union of the divine and human natures in Christ as "the marriage of heaven and earth," which in essence can be considered a realization of the kingdom of God on earth. The church father Athanasius held that "the Saviour's presence in the flesh works our redemption and the salvation of every creature."[5] A modern Roman Catholic theologian, Jean Daniélou, writes about the irrevocable value that belongs to the historical incarnation. According to him, "nothing can ever again divide human nature from Divinity; there is no possibility of a relapse; mankind is essentially saved."[6]

Usually, such incarnational theologies present an organic relationship between the incarnation and creation on the one hand, and the incarnation, the Church and the consummation on the other. The creation is seen as the precondition for the incarnation and the saving work of Christ. By virtue of God's creation, earthly reality is able to enter into the union of the human and the divine. By the same token, the incarnation is seen as "the crowning of the creation," and Christ is sometimes described as the "perfecter of the creation."

The divine-human reality is extended into the world through the Church, which is usually referred to as the "extension" or "prolongation" of the incarnation. The sacramental ministry of the Church is seen as continuing and extending the new reality of the "marriage of heaven and earth" throughout the world. Thus a process of transfiguration is going on which in the end will lead to the glorification of the universe.

This is one way of envisioning the kingdom that has come and is coming. One could say that the formula of the Council of Chalcedon (451) concerning the "hypostatic union" of the two natures in Christ has turned into a theology of history that encompasses the transfiguration of all things through a progressive extension of the incarnation. Theologians in the incarnationist tradition usually fear a heavy emphasis on the atonement, forgiveness, and what they consider to be a one-sided theology of the Word. They see the Reformers as putting too much emphasis on "Word-revelation" vis-à-vis what they would call a "Reality-revelation." Preaching the word of grace is not enough; there must also be a change in the "nature of things." The Reformation churches tend to be oriented toward the street and the public proclamation of the Word. Churches in the Catholic-incarnationist tradition tend to focus on the sanctuary and the mystery of the holy rite.

While such incarnationist theologies contain valid perspectives, the question must still be raised whether they do justice to the significance of the cross and the biblical witness which proclaims that the ascended Lord has sent his Spirit as the true extension of the incarnation. If mankind is essentially saved through the union of the two natures in Christ, why then the cross and why the call to decision? Has the emphasis moved too far from the atonement to the incarnation as *assumptio carnis?*

E. L. Mascall summarizes the issue this way:

> Briefly, the question is whether the re-creation of human nature, which is the *leitmotiv* of the gospel, is to be located in the union of human nature with the Person of the Word in the womb of Mary the Virgin or in the death of the Lord Jesus upon the cross. Is it, in short, Lady Day or Good Friday that is the supreme commemoration of our redemption?[7]

Mascall finally concludes that the cross is essential, even though "we may indeed see the effects of the Incarnation in a gradual supernaturalization of the whole created order."[8] The new creation was fully realized in the hypostatic union of the two natures in Christ, but

> its applicability to us, the re-creation of manhood is initiated only at the moment when, in his death upon the cross, Christ has overcome the powers which enthrall us though they never enthralled him.[9]

Even within the incarnationist theological tradition, the emphases are not always placed or expressed in the same way. Our purpose in this brief survey is not to deal with all the various nuances, but rather to catch a glimpse of the diverse perspectives on the coming of the kingdom.

b. The Cross

A biblical theology of the kingdom must move beyond the doctrine of the incarnation with its glorious affirmation of the union of the divine Logos with human nature in Jesus Christ. The cross of Christ contributes new and crucial perspectives to our understanding of the coming kingdom.

As Paul Minear stated some years ago, "In his effort to describe the kingdom of God, the expositor will fail if he neglects to make the cross the key to the manifest power, wisdom and glory of God."[10]

The apostle Paul wrote to the Christians in Corinth that he had "decided to know nothing among [them] except Jesus Christ and him crucified" (I Cor. 2:2). This seems to be a bit of an overstatement since his letters to them contain discussions on many other themes. The apostle is certainly not preoccupied with death, and Friedrich Nietzsche's dictum that the Christian faith offers a "metaphysics of the hangman" represents one of the worst misunderstandings of the gospel. However, it is true that the cross, as seen and confessed from the perspective of the resurrection, constitutes the heart of the matter. The gospel of the kingdom can also be described as the "word of the cross" (I Cor. 1:18).

In the cross of Christ, the decisive event has taken place: the new order of the kingdom has been established. The Lord of history, who does not want the world to perish in the chaos of sin, confronts the forces of evil and death. God's struggle with all the powers of destructiveness lies at the heart of the drama of history. The cross tells us that sin has been atoned, that there is forgiveness and newness of life, that death has lost its power, and that the forces of evil have been defeated. The crucified One is revealed as the *Christus Victor!* "He disarmed the principalities and the powers and made a public example of them, triumphing over them in him" (or, as some scholars translate, "in it"—i.e., in the cross; Col. 2:15).

Throughout the Scriptures, there is a connection between sin and death. We find it expressed in the account of the Fall in Genesis 3 and in verses such as Ezekiel 18:4, "the soul that sins shall die." In the New Testament we are told that "the wages of sin is death" (Rom. 6:23), and that "the sting of death is sin" (I Cor. 15:56).

Some theologians, particularly the Greek fathers,

have emphasized the aspect of death, while others, particularly those in the tradition of the Reformation, have placed the accent on the reality of sin and guilt. Again, it should be kept in mind that we are not dealing with antithetical positions here, but rather with differences in accent in the development of doctrine. As we saw earlier, the one tradition tends to focus on the theme that the Word became flesh (and thus human nature came to share in eternity), while the other tradition stresses the theme that he who knew no sin was made to be sin for our sake (II Cor. 5:19,21). Both emphases contain important perspectives for a theology of the kingdom.

In the apostle Paul's vision of the end, death is seen as the "last enemy" that must be destroyed (I Cor. 15:26). Chapter 2 of the letter to the Hebrews contains a passage that incorporates several of the themes that have played such a central role in the Church's reflection on the meaning of Christ's redemptive work. First of all, he partook of our nature (v. 14). Secondly, he did that in order that "through death he might destroy him who has the power of death, that is, the devil, and deliver all those who through fear of death were subject to lifelong bondage" (vv. 14-15). And finally, he became "a merciful and faithful high priest in the service of God, to make expiation for the sins of the people" (v. 17).

It is best not to oversystematize these biblical themes in order to defend a rigid doctrinal position. In the cross of Christ, according to Christian confession, God has taken on the power of death itself and has conquered death.

But, the cross also presents us with the rich imagery of the sacrifice which is so deeply rooted in the message of the Old Testament. The drama of the atonement, as portrayed and acted out in the Old Testament sacrificial rite (Lev. 17), tells the story of the deepest and highest dramas of life. The blood represents life in all its passion, impetuousness, and many chaotic contradictions. Where shall the powers of the human passions ever come to rest? Where shall all those chaotic contradictions ever come to a resolution? When the priest casts the blood against the rock of the altar, a profound proclamation concerning the nature and purpose of God is dramatized. God himself will stop the forces that rush toward perdition.

This is the imagery the New Testament writer has in mind when he declares that "without the shedding of blood there is no forgiveness of sins" (Heb. 9:22). In the act of atonement, the righteousness of God confronts the powers and passions of sin and conquers. The cross is the place where God's love and holiness meet. Now the righteousness of the God of love has been manifested. Although we have all fallen short of the glory of God, we "are justified by his grace as a gift, through the redemption which is in Christ Jesus, whom God put forward as an expiation by his blood, to be received by faith. This was to show God's righteousness..." (Rom. 3:23-26).

In the atonement for sin, the righteousness of God has been established upon the earth, the law has been fulfilled, and the foundation of the new order of God which cannot be destroyed by the chaos of sin has been laid. These perspectives are of fundamental significance to a biblical theology of the kingdom. The new order of the kingdom finds its ground and being in the love and justice of God.

Because sin has been atoned, we can become reconciled to God and can receive his forgiveness. But we must move beyond personalistic categories. God is not interested only in humanity; he was in Christ "reconciling the *world* to himself" (II Cor. 5:19). The word of forgiveness contains a glorious truth: "He has delivered us from the dominion of darkness and transferred us to the kingdom of his beloved Son, in whom we have redemption, the forgiveness of sin" (Col. 1:13-14). But we must read on to receive an even broader vision: "For in him all the fulness of God was pleased to dwell, and through him to reconcile to himself all things, whether on earth or in heaven, making peace by the blood of his cross" (v. 20).

The Suffering Servant is revealed as the King of the kingdom. He who "humbled himself and became obedient unto death, even death on a cross," has become highly exalted and on him has been bestowed the name which is above every name (Phil. 2:8-9). The cross and the kingdom are closely related to each other. John Howard Yoder stated this very powerfully when he wrote, "The cross is not a detour or hurdle on the way to the kingdom, nor is it even the way to the kingdom; it is the kingdom come."[11] Yes, but this confession should not prevent us from looking beyond the cross and the resurrection to the ascension and the presence of the kingdom through the fulness of the Spirit.

The atonement for sin has taken place. We can be reconciled to God. There is a word of forgiveness. But the world has not yet been redeemed. The Messiah rules among his enemies (Ps. 110:2). The Reformers spoke about the "reign of the cross" (*regnum crucifixi*) and they used the Latin phrase *tectum sub cruce et sub contrario* to indicate that the kingdom of God is hidden under the cross and the powers that still stand against it. The reality of the cross in history is the reality of human rebellion and resistance to the powers of the new age. But, through the resurrection of Jesus Christ from the dead we are always again "born anew to a living hope" (I Pet. 1:3).

c. The Resurrection

Everything we have said about the cross of Jesus Christ has been said from the perspective of the resurrection. And everything we shall be saying in this section about the resurrection of Jesus Christ presupposes the message of the cross. Our divisions of the biblical materials, necessary as they may sometimes be for theological analysis and educational purposes, must never obscure the inner unity of the message.

The apostle Paul sums up his message as follows:

> For I delivered to you as of first importance what I also received, that Christ died for our sins in accordance with the scriptures, that he was buried, that he was raised on the third day in accordance with the scriptures. (I Cor. 15:3-4)

Herman Ridderbos, who holds that "the coming of the kingdom as the fulfilling eschatological coming of God to the world is the great dynamic principle of Paul's preaching," reminds us that "it is . . . of the greatest importance to see the significance of Christ's death and resurrection, which are the center of Paul's proclamation, as an inseparable unity."[12] Our understanding of the significance of the resurrection in the context of the gospel of the kingdom is decisively influenced by our views on the meaning of the cross.

In the resurrection of Jesus Christ we receive the supreme manifestation of the power of the kingdom. Christ was "designated Son of God in power according to the Spirit of holiness by his resurrection from the dead" (Rom. 1:4). The resurrection is the central breakthrough of the power of the new age. It is both a present reality and a promise for the future.

Those who are "in Christ" share in the new creation: "the old has passed away, behold, the new has come" (II Cor. 5:17). When, through baptism, we share in his death, we shall also share in his resurrection and "walk in newness of life" (Rom. 6:4). In a moving passage the apostle Paul describes how he has given up everything for Christ in order that he might "know him and the power of his resurrection" (Phil. 3:10).

The risen Christ is the "first fruits" of a new humanity (I Cor. 15:20). The first fruits represent the harvest, which will be the new world of the kingdom of God. The resurrection of Jesus Christ is the promise *par excellence* and a preview of things to come. As Adam represents the old humanity, so Christ is inaugurator and representative of the new humanity (I Cor. 15:45 ff.). In the last day, the prophetic vision of the covenant God who dwells with his people shall be fulfilled: "Behold, the dwelling of God is with man. He will dwell with them, and they shall be his people, and God himself will be with them . . ." (Rev. 21:3).

Christ, the risen Lord, is also the

first-born of all creation, for in him all things were created, in heaven and on earth, visible and invisible, whether thrones or dominions or principalities or authorities—all things were created through him and for him. (Col. 1:15–16)

The gospel of the resurrection contains a promise for *all things:* "If Christ has not been raised, then our preaching is in vain and your faith is in vain," writes the apostle Paul to the Corinthians (I Cor. 15:14). But, through the resurrection-faith cosmic visions of God's new order of things are opened up.

d. Ascension/Pentecost

In one sense it can be said that the incarnation has come to an end. In another sense, however, it can be said that the incarnation is being continued through the presence of the Holy Spirit. Both themes are reflected in the biblical witness to the ascension. The ascension speaks of "departure," but not in the sense of space travel. Rather, the ascension witnesses to a "going" that actually represents a new "coming": "I tell you the truth; it is to your advantage that I go away, for if I do not go away, the Counselor will not come to you; but if I go, I will send him to you" (Jn. 16:7).

In a number of New Testament passages the coming of

the promised Spirit is seen in connection with Christ's eventual "departure":

> These things I have spoken to you, while I am still with you. But the Counselor, the Holy Spirit, whom the Father will send in my name, he will teach you all things, and bring to your remembrance all that I have said to you. (Jn. 14:25–26; see also Jn. 7:39)

The closing verses of the Gospel of Luke and the opening section of the Book of Acts (Lk. 24:49–53; Acts 1:4–11) also point to the intimate relationship between the ascension and the coming of the Holy Spirit. As the apostle Peter declared on the day of Pentecost: "Being therefore exalted at the right hand of God, and having received from the Father the promise of the Holy Spirit, he has poured out this which you see and hear" (Acts 2:33). Thus the prophetic vision (Joel 2) has come true: God's Spirit is poured out upon all flesh.

In the Book of Ephesians, with its wide cosmic perspectives, we find one of the most striking statements on this subject. We read that Christ "ascended far above all the heavens, that he might fill all things" (4:10). The imagery of vast distance is combined with the notion of the fulness (*pleroma*) of his presence. The transcendent Lord is very much present in the world. It is therefore not surprising to find an immediate transition in verse 11 with a discussion of the gifts the ascended Lord bestows upon his people for the upbuilding of his Church and its ministry in the world. The *pleroma* of his presence takes place through the power of the Holy Spirit.

According to Calvin "the supreme purpose of the ascension [is] to fill all creation with the *Regnum Christi*."[13] Christ's reign must be established upon the earth. In the Reformed tradition the "marriage of heaven and earth" is not found primarily in the *assumptio carnis*, but in the Christ who through the cross and resurrection has reconciled the world to God, who has overcome the principalities and powers of this world, and who—to use a favored phrase of John Calvin—*spirituali modo* (in the manner and power of the Holy Spirit) is redemptively present in history.

We can also say that the world which has been reconciled to God through the cross and resurrection of Jesus Christ is being sanctified through the power of the Holy Spirit. From the eschatological perspective, that is, from the perspective of the kingdom of God and the transformation of all things, that is the true purpose of God's historical dealings with the world. The old question of whether reconciliation or sanctification is more central to the gospel of Christ is not very meaningful. The biblical witness to reconciliation proclaims that salvation has been accomplished in Christ. The message of sanctification declares that the new creation which has come in Christ is coming into the world through the transforming power of the Holy Spirit.

Our life, together with the whole new creation, is "hid with Christ in God" (Col. 3:3). The ascension further accentuates the message about the hiddenness of the kingdom which we already found in the word of the cross. Sanctification is not yet glorification. Or, perhaps we could say that sanctification is glorification in the form of "fulfillment" or, in the form of "first fruit"—as presence of the kingdom of God in the flesh.

The drama of history, which we described before as the drama of God's struggle with the forces of sin and chaos, continues. As a matter of fact, the biblical witness to the ascension and the coming of the Holy Spirit reveals new perspectives on the meaning of history and the mission of the Christian Church in the world. The interim between the victory of Christ over the powers of this world and his final Parousia constitutes the dispensation of the Spirit and the Church's mission. Time and space are being provided for the proclamation of the gospel of the kingdom and the participation of God's people in his redemptive work in the world.

The account of the ascension in the Book of Acts portrays the disciples as "gazing into heaven" and receiving the message: "Men of Galilee, why do you stand looking into heaven? This Jesus, who was taken up from you into heaven, will come in the same way as you saw him go into heaven" (Acts 1:9–11). The gospel of the ascension and the message of Pentecost point us to the earth, where we are called to live by the power of God's presence and the promise of the Parousia.

e. The Parousia

The consummation of history is portrayed in the New Testament as the Parousia, often referred to as Christ's "second coming." The word "parousia" literally means "presence" or "arrival," and in non-biblical usage it usually referred to a visit by a ruler.

As we have noted earlier, the whole Bible is at heart a witness to God's presence. The Parousia once again points to the divine presence in a new way. The term "second coming" is, therefore, not a very fortunate one. As Paul Minear has stated, "a better distinction is between the coming of God's servant in humiliation and his coming in exaltation, or between the coming of the kingdom in hidden form and the coming in revealed form."[14]

Christ's coming as exalted Lord will mean the resurrection of the dead (Jn. 5:28–29; Acts 24:15; Rev. 20:12–13). Death is swallowed up in victory (I Cor. 15:54). While the final denouement of history will also mean judgment (Rev. 20:11 ff.), the Scriptures leave no doubt that the ultimate victory belongs to the Saviour.

All things will be summed up in Christ (Eph. 1:10). The destiny of the world lies in the new creation which has been revealed in him. The source and destiny of all things are not to be found in the "nature of things." In the final analysis, the whence and whither of existence are revealed in Jesus Christ.

Thy kingdom come. The urgency with which the

Christian community looks toward the coming of the kingdom is also expressed in another prayer: "Come, Lord Jesus!" Parousia means arrival, and in a Christian context it refers to the arrival of the future of the Lord. This future has decisively broken into our present in the coming and saving work of Jesus Christ. It continues to be operative in our midst through the power of the Holy Spirit.

The birth of Jesus Christ, his death upon a cross, his resurrection, his ascension and his sitting at the right hand of God the Father, the outpouring of the Holy Spirit and his coming in exaltation—all these are moments in the coming of the kingdom of God. It makes a difference where one places the emphasis in one's theology and how one treats the unity of the gospel as it witnesses to those various moments in Christ's redemptive work. A church that focuses strongly on the incarnation as *assumptio carnis* will be inclined to see its life, liturgy, and mission in a different light from a church that stresses the ascension and the acts of the Holy Spirit. The manner in which the cross and resurrection are dealt with in one's theology will play an important role in one's approach to history and culture. People who are preoccupied with the Parousia to the neglect of the presence of the kingdom in the here and now tend to develop their very own language and life style.

In short, theological perspectives have their practical consequences. This will become increasingly clear in the following chapters when we deal with the question of the shape of the kingdom in history.

IV *Fulfillment and the Form of the Kingdom*

The kingdom of God comes to us in the form of both "presence" and "promise." These are often referred to as the "already" and the "not yet" aspects of the Christian faith. A few decades ago Oscar Cullmann, using World War II terminology, introduced the notion of D Day and V Day. The great invasion of God's new world has taken place. A new day is dawning. While the final victory has not yet been won, those who have become part of God's great liberation movement in history have no doubt about the eventual outcome.

It is sometimes said that the kingdom is now present as a "small beginning" and that it will develop into a great and glorious future. Perhaps it is better to say that the kingdom is now present in *hidden* form and that what is hidden will be *revealed* (*apocalypsis* = unveiling) in the last day. Redemption has been fully accomplished in Christ and is present in the fulness of the Spirit. But the power of the new age is still engaged in a struggle with the principalities and the powers of this world.

The "already" and the "not yet" aspects of the Christian faith are both essential elements in the hope that it inspires, and they both give that hope its peculiar quality. Rather than being placed in opposition to each other, they must be seen as reinforcements to each other. Through the manifestation of the power of the new age in our midst we

43

experience the future. Thus a foundation is given to our hope, while the foretaste of the future in turn intensifies our longing for the full manifestation of the new heaven and the new earth.

1. THE KINGDOM AS PRESENCE

The Scriptures affirm the *fait accompli* nature of Christ's saving work in many and various ways. He is "Lord of all" (Rom. 10:12). He has overcome the world (Jn. 16:33). All the promises of God are "yes" in him (II Cor. 1:20). The principalities and the powers of this world have been disarmed (Col. 2:15). This is all true *now*. The community of believers confesses him as King of kings and Lord of lords (Rev. 19:16).

The New Testament uses very explicit language when it proclaims the present reality of Christ's rule. The word *pleroma,* both in verb and noun form, is a key term in the New Testament witness. One can hardly do justice to the New Testament message while ignoring the constant emphasis it places on the fulness of God's redemptive presence in Christ and through the Holy Spirit. The notion of "small beginnings" can scarcely do justice to the pleromatic language of the Bible.

We have already seen the remarkable claim in Ephesians 4:10 that Christ has ascended far above all the heavens in order that he might fill all things. A strong emphasis on transcendence is combined with a sense of cosmic nearness. If ever it becomes clear that the Bible does not support a position that plays out the idea of transcendence against the concept of immanence it is in a text like this. In the Scriptures the divine transcendence is always revealed to us in the form of *the mystery of incarnation.* The God who is a "very present help" is the transcendent Lord of the universe. The *pleroma* of the divine presence in history does not diminish the message of transcendence; it witnesses to its mystery.

Christ, the ascended Lord, sends his Spirit, and thus "the fulness of him who fills all in all" dwells in the Church (Eph. 1:23). Christ also dwells in the hearts of his people, and when that happens, they are "filled with all the fulness of God" (Eph. 3:17,19). At Pentecost those who were gathered in Jerusalem were filled with the Spirit, and thus was fulfilled the prophecy of Joel 2 that in the last days the Spirit of God would be poured out on all flesh (Acts 2:17).

All things are made new. Yet, what we are talking about is a rebirth to hope (I Pet. 1:3). Our inheritance is "kept in heaven" (I Pet. 1:4); our new life is "hid with Christ in God" (Col. 3:3). The christological and pneumatological realism that confronts us in the Scriptures is through and through eschatological in nature. Fulfillment is a futuristic reality. The experience of the *pleroma* of God is not yet the kingdom of God, just as sanctification is not yet glorification. But by the same token it is nothing less than the presence of the power of the kingdom itself. However, until the principalities and the powers of this world, which have been dethroned as ruling powers, have been totally subjected to God's dominion, the presence of the kingdom will be manifested in the form of "signs." The signs of the kingdom, like Jesus' ministry of healing or the rebirth of a human heart, are full of the reality they signify, namely, the power of the new age.

2. THE KINGDOM AS PROMISE

In Jesus Christ all the promises of God are "Yes"; they *have* been fulfilled. That does not mean, however, that as Christians we no longer live by promise. Quite to the contrary, fulfillment means that in Christ the promises have been *confirmed* and that now more than ever we live by the promises of God. We are saved in hope (Rom. 8:24).

In the name of fulfillment Christians have often made false claims, particularly vis-à-vis the Jewish people. On the basis of the promise-fulfillment scheme, which certainly expresses a fundamental truth, the impression has been created that the people of the old covenant had only promises, as if there was no presence of the kingdom among them, and that we Christians now have the "real thing," as if we no longer live by promise. The Christian view of fulfillment and the conviction that in Jesus Christ the kingdom of God has broken through in a decisive way, definitely make a difference in the way we experience and witness to our expectation. But it should never be forgotten that as Christians we share with the Jews the vision about the coming of the Lord and his kingdom. Because of our faith in Christ, we believe that the promises of God have received a new confirmation and his coming kingdom has received a new and firm foundation, but that in no way eliminates the fact that Christians are people who have become "partakers of the promise" with the people of Israel (Eph. 3:6). We must not behave as if we have left the realm of promise behind and have arrived at our destination.

Come, Lord Jesus! The Christian faith still finds expression in a prayer of profound yearning. Thus we join the saints and visionaries of old who have prayed with deep urgency for the Lord to hasten the day of his coming. Those who have been grasped by the vision of the new heaven and the new earth cannot but become deeply aware of the "not yet." Sometimes it may seem that the anti-forces are completely in charge. Longing is very much part of the Christian life.

Nevertheless, that longing does not find its source in the absence of the kingdom. Our future expectation is not rooted in a sense of the emptiness and futility of the world, but rather in the confession of the presence of the kingdom. A Christian hope that is based on a belief in the presence of the kingdom will not soon become escapist and otherworldly. Ours is not a passive hope. The power of the new age is being manifested in history; God is establishing his kingdom upon the earth; there is fulfillment and we receive a foretaste of the future. Therefore, hope becomes expressed in our mission to the world. Christians do not want to stop the world so that they can get off. Instead, like Abraham, they live as sojourners in the land of promise (Heb. 11:9).

The Holy Spirit is called "the guarantee of our inheritance until we acquire possession of it" (Eph. 1:14). In the meantime we are sealed with "the promised Holy Spirit" or, as the Greek could also be rendered, with "the Holy Spirit of promise" (Eph. 1:13). Both translations express a fundamental insight of the Christian faith. The prophecy has been fulfilled; the promised Spirit has been poured out on the day of Pentecost. Now we live by the power of the Spirit of promise.

The very presence of the Spirit fills all of life with a sense of anticipation. In a passage that focuses on "the things of the Spirit" (Rom. 8:5), the apostle Paul declares that the whole creation is waiting with eager longing "to be set free from its bondage to decay and obtain the glorious liberty of the children of God" (Rom. 8:21). In other words, when the ascended Christ is present in the fulness (*pleroma*) of his redemption, all of existence becomes qualified by the coming of the future of the Lord. The whole creation is reaching out for the consummation of all things. The cosmos is pregnant with promise. In the words of Jürgen Moltmann, "hope becomes realistic and reality hopeful."[1]

3. LIVING BETWEEN THE TIMES

When the "already" of the kingdom is emphasized to the neglect of the "not yet," the Church tends to lose its eschatological perspective and to settle down in the world. Soon it becomes inflicted with a triumphalistic spirit. Some Christians become preoccupied with ambitious programs that are designed to put the teachings of the gospel into practice and to produce a new social-political order in accordance with the principles of the kingdom of God. The French lay theologian and social critic Jacques Ellul, for instance, complains that many Protestant intellectuals today are treating God's "Yes" to the world in Jesus Christ as if it involved a cancellation of his "No."[2]

On the other hand, when the "not yet" is stressed at the expense of the "already," the world tends to be viewed as being under the rule of Satan, and a spirit of escapism and other-worldliness often prevails. There is much talk about heaven and the hopelessness of any human efforts to establish a more just social order. Between these two extremes of an uncritical world acceptance and a spiritualizing world flight, one finds a wide spectrum of positions, each accentuating the dialectic between the "already" and the "not yet" in its own particular way.

The theologies of Luther and Calvin, as set forth by T. F. Torrance in his valuable study *Kingdom and Church*, present an interesting illustration of how such differences in accent affect one's overall approach to the world and the issues of society. After pointing to the basic visions the various Reformation theologians had in common, Torrance describes the difference between Luther and Calvin as follows:

> Broadly speaking, their divergence may be characterized by saying that while Lutheran eschatology was mainly an eschatology of judgement, going back to early Latin Fathers like Cyprian with their emphasis on the decay and the collapse of the world, Reformed eschatology was mainly an eschatology of the resurrection, going back to the early Greek Fathers with their emphasis upon the renewal of the world through the Incarnation of Christ.[3]

Both Luther and Calvin present a theology of the cross and the resurrection, but they place different emphases on how the cross and the resurrection affect the form the kingdom of God assumes in history.

The term "kingdom of the Devil" recurs regularly in Luther's writings, while Calvin places strong emphasis on the reign of Christ (*regnum Christi*) as the form in which the reign of God (*regnum Dei*) is exercised upon the earth and bears fruit. Both retained a dynamic eschatological perspective, but while Luther often used apocalyptic language to describe the course of history, Calvin saw the Holy Spirit as operating in history, thus giving a preliminary form to the kingdom of Christ in the world. In short, Luther had a more difficult time than Calvin relating his eschatological vision to the historical realities of his day. Or, as Roger Shinn has expressed it, Luther "was unable to develop a constructive theology for this-worldly hope."[4] His two-kingdom doctrine, which tended to keep the Church out of the social-economic and political spheres, was a logical result of the manner in which he laid the accent between the "already" and the "not yet."

Similar dynamics have been at the heart of the theological debates in recent decades about the social implications of the gospel and the mandate of Christian mission. The World Council of Churches, which has played a central role in those debates, has moved through a variety of phases in its pronouncements on these matters. It should be emphasized once again that we are not talking about radical switches in position, but rather about changes in emphasis.

In 1947, Dr. W. A. Visser 't Hooft, then General Secretary of the WCC, published the Dutch edition of his book *The Kingship of Christ*. Following Oscar Cullmann's thesis in his book *Christ and Time*, Visser 't Hooft strongly emphasized that Christ is Lord over both the Church and the world, and developed a Christocentric approach to the State. In the believing community Christ is confessed as Head and served as Lord, while the powers of this world do not recognize his lordship. Where the lordship of Christ is not confessed, the powers of this world, and particularly those powers that are operative in the State, tend to deify themselves and to become demonic in their functions. However, none of this can eliminate the fact that they have lost their final authority and will in the end be under the dominion of the *regnum Christi*.

From its earliest days, the WCC has had a keen interest in applying the message of the gospel to world issues. Dealing with the theme "Christ, the Hope of the World" in 1954, the Evanston Assembly sought to develop an eschatology that did equal justice to the biblical dimensions of "already" and "not yet." However, at that time when European theologians still had a dominant influence in the Council, there were already expressions of concern that a disproportionate emphasis was being placed on the present reality of Christian hope as against the ultimate hope.

Since the 1960s much has been written about shifts in emphasis in WCC pronouncements on the life and mission of the Church. According to some commentators the turning point occurred at the World Conference on Church and Society, held in Geneva in 1966. The discussions on "a responsible society" were increasingly conducted in the terminology of a theology of revolution. The WCC itself was undergoing profound internal changes as Third World Christians played an increasingly important role in its leadership and conferences. Urgent and often militant demands for radical changes in the world's social-economic order were being heard from all sides. The WCC, building on its confession of the lordship of Christ and God's liberating activity in the world, sought to respond with a legitimate biblical concern for justice and the need for new approaches to societal problems.

During the 1968 Uppsala Assembly it seemed to many WCC participants and observers that the biblical dialectic of "already" and "not yet" was being reduced to one-sided and ideologically inspired theories of world improvement. Latin American liberation theologians, with their penchant for the terminology of Marxist social analysis combined with a strong emphasis on the theme of "humanization," helped to convince many old and some new critics of the WCC that it had exchanged the biblical message of the kingdom of God for a "this-worldly" philosophy of social-economic development.

Anyone who has read the actual documents issued by WCC-sponsored conferences during the past decade knows, as the Dutch theologian Hendrikus Berkhof has pointed out on various occasions, that it is more a matter of "small print" versus "large print" than a question of total neglect of valid gospel dimensions. The strategy to deal with biblical and dialectical questions in terms of small and large print is hardly an exclusive temptation of "ecumenicals." Evangelicals too have had long experience in such exercises! The other side of an issue is not totally ignored; it is merely incorporated into the "small print" sections of a document.

Now there are indications that a new shift in emphasis is occurring within the WCC. Its Commission on World Mission and Evangelism, which is planning a major conference in Melbourne, Australia, in 1980, has chosen the theme "Thy Kingdom Come" for its studies and deliberations. The preliminary literature on the conference strikes an apocalyptic note that seems somewhat out of tune with recent pronouncements on the churches' responsibility to help change society. One senses an implicit confession that some of the statements issued in recent years were overly optimistic about the prospects for the human condition and the impact the churches could have in bringing about major changes in society. The principalities and the powers of this world, the forces of social-economic and political self-interest, and the stubborn resistance to change proved to be far more powerful than some ecumenical pronouncements had intimated.

The exodus theme of yesteryear is apparently being replaced by the wilderness theme, and the praxis of prayer for the coming of God's kingdom now seems to be stressed as much as the political praxis to build a new world order. Does the new apocalyptic tone mean that the WCC is withdrawing from its commitment to relate the gospel to the world's distressing needs? This does not seem likely.

Apocalypticism does not *ipso facto* lead to world escape. As we have seen earlier, such movements are usually imbued with a spirit of world-negation, but this can be a creative negation which finds its source in an affirmation of the coming future of the Lord. The apocalypticist is often the rebel, who in the words of Albert Camus is a person who dares to say "No," but whose soul may be on fire with the vision of a new world.

Our present era is ripe for a resurgence of apocalyptic visions. The horsemen of the Book of Revelation have appeared on the horizon of contemporary history. As Donald Sneen states in his book *Visions of Hope:*

> Stability of the times and interest in apocalyptic literature are in inverse ratio. The 20th century is an age of apocalyptic birth pangs. The arms race and a possible nuclear holocaust threaten all life on our planet . . . The melting of the arctic ice cap, depletion of the earth's ozone layer, theft of plutonium by terrorists, and ill-fated experimentation with weather modification are additional threats.[5]

The early Christians envisaged cataclysmic events of a different nature, but the spirit which caused some of them to view the world in terms of a terminal illness which would eventually lead to decay and self-destruction, was quite similar to the mood among many concerned people today. The "not yet" dimension of the gospel of the kingdom consumes their souls. Nothing less than a divine intervention of cosmic proportions will provide the answer for history. Apocalyptic hope is expressed in prophetic protest against the present system and all the oppressive structures of society.

George Hunsinger stands in a long apocalyptic tradition when he writes in *Sojourners* magazine:

We live in evil times. The time is coming and now is when darkness shall cover the face of the earth. The time is coming and now is when militarism is out of control, when there are wars and rumors of wars, when there are famines and when there is torture, when ecological disaster is impending, when the struggle against racism and sexism is subsiding, when a so-called mild recession is being planned to retard inflation while millions of men and women are out of work, when politicians make promises they can not keep, because the very structure of our economic system prevents them from keeping them, when the apparatus of national security has become the greatest threat to national security, and when there seems to be little hope for our children and our world that the world can be stayed from destroying itself.[6]

This is not a message of despair because Hunsinger's sermon, entitled "The Shadow and the Promise," ends on a note of great hope. It is the voice of one crying in the wilderness to a world that seems to be in pursuit of perdition. Many others have voiced similar cries throughout the centuries: the Montanists in the 2nd century, the Anabaptists in the 16th century, the Blumhardts in the 19th century, to mention only a few. Their eschatological vision inspired the vehemence of their protest.

Not only is the nature of our hope at stake in these issues, but also the shape of our witness in the world. Can it be anything but the shape of the cross? What does it really mean to live in this present age as a people of hope?

In 1970, while reflecting on his book *Theology of Hope,* which had been published five years earlier, Jürgen Moltmann expressed the feeling that he had left his readers "in the lurch as regards the practice of hope." He further observed how after having written his "theology of hope" he felt a need to move deeper into "political theology." We are not called to proclaim an abstract theory of hope, but a present kingdom, a future in the process of becoming. In the same context, Moltmann observes that he also wanted to reflect more intensely than he had before on the meaning of the cross for theology, the Church, and society.[7] His more recent writings embody the insights gained from those reflections.

The World Council's Commission on World Mission and Evangelism has also announced that at their 1980 meeting in Melbourne, the theme "Thy Kingdom Come" will be approached from the perspective of the cross and the message of the Suffering Servant. Again, this in no way implies that the WCC is ready to abandon its social witness and its call for a just world order. It does mean, it seems to me, that the WCC, together with many other Christians— both in the so-called ecumenical and evangelical camps— is still searching for a biblical theology and an ecumenical witness that creatively incorporate the gospel dimensions of the coming kingdom.

4. SIGNS OF THE KINGDOM

The preceding section concluded with a strong note on the reality of the cross. Blaise Pascal wrote that Jesus Christ will be in agony till the end of the age. *That* we can understand, for all around us we observe the evidences of the reality of the cross.

How then shall we speak about the "already" in days like these? As we seek to give an account of the hope that is in us (I Pet. 3:15), do we dare, in times such as these, declare to the world that the *pleroma* of Christ's rule dwells in our midst? Can we really with any degree of credibility confess Christ as King of kings and Lord of lords?

The question of messianic fulfillment is, of course, the key issue in Christian-Jewish conversations. For instance, when Harvey Cox, in his book *The Secular City*, presented the thesis that certain movements and events in our time can be identified as the breaking in of the kingdom of God, the Jewish participants in the debate that followed zeroed in on precisely this question: Can it be meaningfully stated in any sense that the messianic era has been inaugurated and that the kingdom of God is present in our world?[8] In encounters with the Jewish people, the Church is consistently called upon to account for the fact that it finds the foundation of its hope in the belief that the kingdom is present in history. Judaism confronts Christians with the perennially troubling question about where in her midst the signs of the kingdom, as proclaimed in the prophetic vision, are manifested. The Jewish people, more than anyone else, remind the Church of the "not yet" of the kingdom of God and challenge her to justify her claims. This is why a genuine encounter with Judaism always serves as a healthy antidote against all sorts of Christian triumphalisms.

But within the Christian community as well, a lively debate is going on about the shape of the kingdom of God in history.[9] Those who put strong emphasis on the cross as the fundamental reality by which history must be understood, are inclined to interpret the nature and mission of the Church in terms of countersign, resistance, conflict with the established order, and protest. In short, they are extremely skeptical about any Christian claims that there are embodiments of the kingdom in this world so full of misery, injustice, and oppression.

Karl Löwith once wrote that "nothing else than the life and death of Jesus Christ, the 'Suffering Servant' who was deserted and crucified, can be a standard of a Christian understanding of the world's history."[10] But what then about the resurrection? One of the most helpful discussions on history in terms of the cross and resurrection of Jesus Christ can be found in Hendrikus Berkhof's book *Christ the Meaning of History*. It contains a chapter entitled "Christ, the Crucified One in History," which discusses the counterforces to the power and values of the kingdom of God. Then, in the next chapter, "Christ, the Risen One in History," he points to the positive signs of the resurrection in the midst of the historical realities of our day.

Berkhof stresses the point that "in the present dispensation there is no balance between cross and resurrection, let alone an ascendancy of the resurrection."[11] We live "between the times." The veil which hides from our eyes the actual victory of Christ over the powers of sin and death has not been finally removed. We live in the dispensation of fulfillment, which implies concealment of the kingdom's presence in the midst of a sinful world. Fulfillment is not yet consummation.

"Cross and resurrection are not active in the same history-making manner," writes Berkhof, and continues:

> This is connected with their different place and function in salvation-history. The cross is central to the history of our old guilty world which died with the erection of the cross. For that reason the suffering and death of Jesus are vividly described in the Gospels, in much detail and in concrete terms. It is different with the resurrection. It is the breakthrough of God's new world which is radically different from the old.[12]

In order to understand the New Testament witness to the redemptive realities "between the times," we should pay careful attention to such terms as "guarantee," "first fruits," and "signs." Together they form a cluster of ideas that give us deeper insight into the meaning of fulfillment. They are at the heart of the New Testament pneumatology.

Pentecost has happened, the Holy Spirit has been poured out, and now we experience the "first fruits" of the Spirit. In the magnificent passage in Romans 8 where the apostle Paul describes the whole creation as reaching out for the divinely appointed destiny of all things *because* of the presence of the Holy Spirit, we read that "not only the creation, but we ourselves, who have the first fruits of Spirit, groan inwardly as we wait for adoption as sons, the redemption of our bodies" (v. 24)!

In other words, in the present dispensation fulfillment and the *pleroma* of the Spirit come to us in the form of "first fruits." It would be a mistake to place the emphasis here on the "smallness" of the "beginning" of the presence of God's renewing power. In the Old Testament the first fruits are *representative* of the whole harvest, and that is also the idea conveyed by the New Testament.

In the interim we are "sealed" by the Spirit which is given us as a "guarantee" (II Cor. 1:22; 5:5). We return to the words in Ephesians 1:13–14 which we noted before:

> In him you also, who have heard the word of truth, the gospel of your salvation, and have believed in him, were sealed with the promised Holy Spirit (or, the Holy Spirit of promise), which is the guarantee of our inheritance until we acquire possession of it, to the praise of his glory.

Apparently, a key function of the Spirit "between the times" is to preserve, guide, and prepare existence for the coming of the Day of the Lord.

We live by spiritual realities. This does not mean that reality should be spiritualized. Far from it! The Spirit has been poured out upon all flesh. The Holy Spirit is operative, not only in the hearts of people, but in the history of the world. The end of the ways of God is still corporeality. God is dealing with the stuff of this earth, because he remains faithful to his creation and is saving it. The great breakthrough of God's new creation has occurred in the power of the resurrection. Christ has ascended far above all the heavens that through the Spirit he might fill all things. In the "first fruits" the great harvest of the kingdom of God is represented in our midst.

Whenever breakthroughs of the kingdom occur, signs are established upon the earth. The Gospel of John in particular refers to Jesus' saving acts as "signs." They are signs of the kingdom pointing to the reality of the new world by revealing the power of that reality. When Jesus healed a person, this was a sign of *shalom*, a foretaste of the time when humanity and the world shall be whole. When Jesus fed people, that too was a sign of the new tomorrow, a present manifestation of the promise that humanity shall not always live in a world where some people starve in the midst of abundance. When a person found forgiveness in the presence of Jesus, it was a sign of the day when all captivity shall be made captive by the power of God. And when a person, who had gained his wealth in ways that are not in accordance with the laws of the kingdom, decided to pay compensation to those whom he had wronged, that was a sign of a new order of things in which justice and righteousness shall prevail. Moltmann correctly points out that "the talk about God's 'signs and wonders' is rooted in the Deuteronomistic view of history."[13] Signs occur when the Lord acts in history.

Today, through the work of the Holy Spirit, we still see signs of the future that is being realized. The Bible warns us that we must expect both the positive and negative signs of the kingdom to be manifested in growing intensity. There will be wars, famine, and persecution. But also, the gospel of the kingdom will be preached throughout the earth (Mt. 24), lives will be transformed, laws will be passed that will provide a measure of justice to those who have been oppressed, and in the midst of the chaos of sin, life will be preserved, guided, and prepared for the coming of the Day of the Lord.

These signs must not be confused with the reality they signify, for they are not the kingdom. However, they are not mere symbols either, for they are charged with the *power* of the reality they signify. We tend to become restless with the message about signs; we want quick resolutions to the problems of the world. On the one hand, the presence of the Spirit is meant to fill us with a holy restlessness about things as they are. The Spirit is never an advocate for the *status quo*. He turns people into visionaries and dreamers (Acts 2). On the other hand, the

Spirit fills us with hope and persistence when quick results and easy resolutions are not available. The signpost ought not to be confused with the destiny; it beckons us to journey on. We remain "pilgrims of the future."

Thus we live in the tension of the "already" and the "not yet." The tension is part of the journey of faith. Any attempt to resolve the tension prematurely, either by claiming possession of that which must be received in the form of promise and first fruits, or by seeking to flee the present world and its responsibilities into a spiritualized futurism will mean loss of essential elements of the gospel of the kingdom. We wait for a new heaven and a new earth, but we also seek to hasten it (II Pet. 3:11–13).

5. THE CONSUMMATION: CONTINUITY/DISCONTINUITY

The sign represents the reality signified. The very future of the Lord is in our midst. But how shall we conceive of the movement from fulfillment to consummation, and what is the relationship between the history we experience and the new creation which is beyond our comprehension? According to I John 3:2, "it does not yet appear what we shall be." The future of the Lord holds its surprises.

There are passages in the Bible, particularly in the parables, which suggest a gradual development from the kingdom that is now present to the consummation that is yet to come. In Matthew 13, for instance, we find the so-called parables of growth: the parable of the sower, the wheat and the tares, the mustard seed, and the leaven. They are certainly parables of hope and expectation. They also proclaim the miracle-nature of what God is doing in the world. The breakthroughs of the kingdom of God do give a sense of the evolvement of his future in the present time. It could be said that the whole Bible is witness to a series of divine breakthroughs: the exodus, the giving of the Torah, deliverances in times of crisis, the prophetic testimony, God's coming in Christ, the outpouring of the Spirit, and the divine presence in our own history.

Yet, the idea of a gradual process whereby the present is evolving into the future of the kingdom of God can easily be distorted. Nineteenth-century liberalism distorted it with its belief in progress and in the gradual growth of goodness on earth. As H. Richard Niebuhr has stated so well:

> the idea of the kingdom was robbed of its dialectical element. It was all fulfillment of promise without judgment. It was thought to be growing out of the present so that no great crisis needed to intervene between the order of grace and the order of glory. In its one-sided view of progress which saw the growth of the wheat but not that of the tares, the gathering of the grain but not the burning of the chaff, this liberalism was indeed naively optimistic.[14]

The Bible indicates that there will be an intensifying of the conflict as the power of God's future breaks into the present world and challenges the powers that be. We already referred to the negative signs which, together with the positive signs of the end time, will grow in intensity: war, famine, oppression, apostasy, and so forth (Mt. 24). The final conflict is between the rule of Christ and "the principalities and the powers—the world rulers of this present darkness—the spiritual hosts of wickedness" (Eph. 6:12). And, as Alfred Krass has observed, "whenever God's kingdom is being established the 'power of lawlessness' (II Thess. 2:3ff) is also seeking to do its work."[15]

Over against the texts portraying a gradual process of the growth of the kingdom one can set apocalyptic passages with their visions of a cataclysmic break between the present and the final breakthrough of the kingdom. II Peter 3:5 ff. presents a graphic illustration: "the day of the Lord will come like a thief, and then the heavens will pass away with a loud noise, and the elements will be dissolved with fire, and the earth and the works that are upon it will be burned up."

Such passages may lead one to conclude that there will be a total and absolute break between the present and the future kingdom. "There is no continuity," declares Jacques Ellul, "between our history and the kingdom, anymore than there is a continuity between our earthly life and our resurrected life."[16] That view, it would seem, could lead to a one-sidedness which ought to be avoided as carefully as the overly optimistic view about continuous development. (There are indications in Ellul's own works that he did not mean that in an absolute way.)

The Book of Revelation does not hold that the works of humanity will be "burned up." Rather, we are told that those who die in the Lord are blessed and that their deeds do follow them (ch. 14:13). Even the glories of the kings of the earth and the honor of the nations will be brought into the New Jerusalem (ch. 21:24,26). H. Berkhof, whose book *Christ the Meaning of History* contains an extremely helpful discussion on this matter of discontinuity and continuity in the consummation, concludes that "we are forced into the grateful acknowledgement that in the glorification of this world God will add to what has been realized of the liberation of human existence."[17]

None of our achievements, programs and projects, or our social actions, campaigns and crusades, should be absolutized as if they constituted the kingdom itself. Yet, by the grace of God, the fruits of our labors, ministries, and mission can become part of God's recreative work. The time of fulfillment between Pentecost and the Parousia is the dispensation of the Spirit and the apostolate of the Church.

However, before we discuss the various implications of this apostolate, we will pause in the next chapter for some historical reflection. As the Christian Church has wrestled with the question of the kingdom of God, it has pursued some paths that have headed in the wrong direction. Now that kingdom theology is once again moving to the forefront of Christian reflection, lessons from history might prevent us from taking these same directions.

V Lessons from History

We have noted that the life of Christian faith and obedience must be lived in the tension of the "already" and the "not yet." One does not have to probe very deeply into the history of the Christian Church to discover that those who confessed Christ as Lord were rarely able to deal creatively with these tensions. Time and time again they succumbed to the temptation to resolve the tensions prematurely, either by claiming for the Church what belongs to the kingdom, or by claiming for the present world what belongs to the world to come, or by confining the realm of the kingdom either to the inner life or to the future.

The early Christians lived from profound eschatological expectations. When the Church lost its eschatological perspective, it soon began making excessive claims for itself. This happened first with respect to the relationship between the Church and the Jewish people. "We are the new Israel!" said the Christians, implying that they had replaced the Jews with whom God no longer was supposed to have any covenant dealings. Forgetting that Christians are really people who have become "partakers of the promise" with the people of Israel (Eph. 3:6), Christians did exactly what Paul, in Romans 11, warned them not to do: they boasted about their status vis-à-vis Israel. The branches that had been grafted into the trunk of Israel behaved as if they were the roots that supported the tree.

Thus began the tragic process which caused the Church to lose contact with its very roots in Judaism.

After the Church had once claimed the status of the "New Israel," it was only a short step to claiming to be the New Jerusalem as well. Christians began to interpret the life of the Church as *the* expression or even realization of the kingdom of God on earth. According to J. E. Fison, the Church "transferred the New Testament emphasis upon a present and future kingdom of God upon earth to a present Church on earth and a distinctly remote future kingdom in heaven."[1]

By the 4th century, Constantine had made Christianity the official religion of the empire. While there is no agreement among interpreters of St. Augustine (354–430) as to how far Augustine went in making the Church and the kingdom identical, there is no doubt that those who followed him frequently used his writings to defend the thoroughly unscriptural equation of the kingdom with the Church which, says Fison, "can so easily involve an apotheosis of an institution."[2]

Through a process of acculturation, the Church increasingly accommodated itself to the surrounding culture, thus becoming this-worldly in the wrong way. The "pilgrims of the future" became the established Church. Those who protested these developments usually did so not in the name of a biblical this-worldliness, which is grounded in the creation, the incarnation, and the presence of the kingdom in the power of the Holy Spirit, but rather by internalizing the kingdom, thus removing it from the world of daily experiences.

Christian theology tends to go to extremes as movements of thought that emerge in reaction against one-sided interpretations of Scripture often do by adapting a stance on the opposite pole of the theological spectrum. For instance, the theologies of Friedrich Schleiermacher and Albert Ritschl, which, influenced by Kant's philosophy, gave the kingdom a thoroughly ethical and this-worldly interpretation, were followed by the early dialectical theology with its strong existential emphasis. This eventually found its culmination in the existentialist theology of Rudolf Bultmann, in which "the moment of decision" swallows up the eschatological dimensions of the gospel and gives ultimate meaning to history.[3] Today, as we have pointed out several times, we see a new search going on for a theology of the kingdom of God that will do justice to the social and political implications of the gospel. In the development of such a theology, three areas should receive particular attention. They involve the relationship of the kingdom of God to the Church, the world, and the inner life.

1. KINGDOM AND CHURCH

Since the medieval period, the equation of the kingdom of God with the Church has been quite common, particularly in the Catholic tradition. During the Reformation, serious questions were raised about this position. Through insights gained from a rediscovery of biblical eschatology, the Reformers began once again to write theology in dynamic historical categories. They viewed history in terms of continual reformation as the pilgrim people of God journey toward the future of the kingdom.

Still, a close relationship between the Church and the kingdom was maintained, sometimes even appearing to approximate a new identification between Church and kingdom. Yet, whatever difficulties the Reformers may have had in formulating the nature of the relationship, they never lost sight of the problems posed by interpreting the kingdom in triumphalistic ecclesiastical terms.

On this question, as on so many others, a radical change of perspective has been occurring among Roman Catholic theologians and philosophers. Jacques Maritain, for instance, believed that the kingdom has already come in the form of the Church, but that it is "the kingdom in the state of pilgrimage and crucifixion."[4] Such a view will not easily lead to grandiose claims about the nature of the Church; it opens wide the doors to the eschatological perspective. Chapter seven of the *Constitution on the Church*, issued by the Second Vatican Council, is entitled "The Eschatological Nature of the Pilgrim Church and her Union with the Heavenly Church." It clearly states:

> that until there is a new heaven and a new earth where justice dwells, the pilgrim Church in her sacraments and institutions which pertain to this present time, takes on the appearance of this passing world. She herself dwells among creatures who groan and travail in pain until now and await the revelation of the sons of God.[5]

Writers in the Eastern Orthodox tradition sometimes describe the Church in language that suggests that the Church rather than the world is the purpose and end of God's saving activity. "It may be said," wrote Sergius Bulgakov, "that the Church was the eternal end and the foundation of creation."[6] Thus it seems as if both christology and the gospel of the kingdom have been swallowed up by ecclesiology.

Father George Khodr, in an article in the *International Review of Mission*, gives a more modest appraisal of the nature of the Church. But he also calls the Church "the cosmos in process of transformation," and then adds:

> It is the visible expression of the promise of the kingdom as well as the threshold of this kingdom. It is the hope offered now as something in which we are already participating in the sacraments. In that sense, the Church is already heaven on earth.[7]

When the focus is drawn so sharply on the mystery that takes place in the Church, one begins to wonder whether the vision of the Church's mission in the world will still be maintained.

Is it not better to refer to the Church in even more modest terms and call it a *sign* of the kingdom? In a very special way the power of the new age is manifested in the Church, and it can rightly be said that the Church is at the center of God's redemptive dealings with the world. Such a perception, however, should not lead to a church-centered theology, but rather should become part of a kingdom-oriented theology.

God has so loved the *world* that he has sent his Son. And it is because of that same love for the world that today he sends the Church. In serving the world, the Church serves the kingdom. In the consummation of all things, a temple will no longer be needed (Rev. 21:22), and the Son will deliver the kingdom to the Father (I Cor. 15:24). The messianic community and the Messiah have served their purpose in God's historical-eschatological dealings with the world. Then God will be all in all; his *shalom* will reign upon the earth.

To say that the Church is a sign of the kingdom does not mean that one has a low view of the Church. As was stressed already, the Church is seen as very central in God's dealings with the world. Church and kingdom are not identical to each other, nor are they antithetical to each other. During the opening years of this century, A. Loisy voiced the complaint that Jesus announced the kingdom, but that we ended up with the Church. The Church was then viewed as an unfortunate development that was unforeseen by Jesus, as Albert Schweitzer and his followers later claimed. We were promised the kingdom but that dream did not materialize.

As Christians, we confess that the signs of the kingdom are indeed in our midst. These are not empty signs, for in them the power of the new age is manifested. In that sense the kingdom of God is realized upon the earth. However, in view of the eschatological expectation of the consummation it is better not to use the term "realized eschatology."

The Church must be understood from the perspective of the kingdom; the kingdom should not be interpreted exclusively in terms of the Church. The Church is an eschatological community. It exists for the sake of the kingdom. It proclaims the breakthroughs of the future of the Lord and the vision of the new heaven and the new earth. Through the Word and the sacraments the new creation is present in the power of the Spirit.

The sacraments are celebrations of hope, as well as commemorations of Christ's redemptive ministry. They are "sacraments of inaugurated eschatology" (Neville Clarke). "Like the proclamation of the gospel of the last days," writes Jürgen Moltmann in his work *The Church in the Power of the Spirit,*

> Christian baptism is eschatology put into practice. It manifests the advent of the coming God through Christ in human life and is the sign of Life's conversion to the life of Easter. Like the proclamation of the gospel of the last days, Christian baptism is Christian hope in action.[8]

Moltmann's section on the Lord's supper is entitled "The Sign of Remembered Hope." In this section the kingdom perspective is very pronounced:

> The Lord's supper is, with inner, factual cogency, the expression of the eschatological history of Christ—that is to say, the dawn of the kingdom of God in his self-giving and his resurrection from the dead. The fellowship with Christ made effective in the supper is the fellowship of the coming kingdom, and the fellowship of the kingdom of God is present in the fellowship of Christ in the midst of the history of evil and suffering. The Lord's supper is the eschatological sign of the coming kingdom in history.[9]

At heart, the mission of the Church is also an expression of Christian hope, an entering into the mission of Christ himself. It is the mission of those who know that the kingdom involves the future of all humanity and the recreation of all things. The proclamation of the gospel of the kingdom throughout the whole world is one of the great signs of the end (Mt. 24:14). Furthermore, through the mission of the Church in the power of the Holy Spirit, new signs of the kingdom are established upon the earth.

The signs of the new age are particularly manifested in the Church, but not exclusively so. The Spirit is also at work in the world. The signs of the kingdom in the world may well be the fruit of the proclamation of the gospel of the kingdom by the Church, even though, in particular cases, this relationship is often not self-evident. The gospel of the kingdom has an impact upon the nations where it is preached. In a very tentative and fragmentary way it bears fruit and becomes embodied in the cultural and social-political life of a people. We ought to be careful not to use phrases like a "Christian nation" in too uncritical a fashion. But on the other hand, we ought not to dismiss the impact of the gosepl too quickly by saying that it is only a thin veneer covering the surface of societies. We know from history what happens when this thin veneer is removed and the demonic forces just below the surface break through. Auschwitz has become the horrendous symbol of a "Christian nation" seeking to become *Judenrein* and celebrating the ancient paganism that still lies buried in the Western soul.

The Lord of history is active in the world. We should not try to draw all redemptive realities into the Church. The language we use in our witness and confessional statements should be carefully examined. For instance, in 1975 the Reformed Church in America and the Christian Reformed Church issued a joint "Evangelism Manifesto" for study in their churches. The message of the kingdom is at the core of the whole document. In the context of contemporary discussions on evangelism that must be considered a significant contribution. Yet, we read in this "Manifesto" that the Spirit has been poured out upon the Church, instead of upon "all flesh." It refers to "the signs of God's kingdom among his people" rather than in the world, and Christians are portrayed as people who are actively concerned about "the full deliverance and restoration of all to whom the gospel is addressed" rather than the recreation of "all things."

The kingdom must not be ecclesiasticized. Nor should it be secularized. To the latter concern we must now turn.

2. KINGDOM AND WORLD

The kingdom of God is not *from* this world (Jn. 18:36). In the last analysis the kingdom belongs to the new world that comes "from heaven" (Rev. 21:2). Yet, the kingdom of God is definitely *for* this world and is very much present *in* this world. The realm of the kingdom is, in essence, the reality of God's sovereign and redeeming grace. According to the biblical witness, the most joyful truth about the "other world" is that it has entered this world and qualifies it by its presence.

In the mystery of the kingdom a "marriage of heaven and earth" takes place. The new world of God's tomorrow is operative in our midst through the transforming power of the Holy Spirit. Through his redeeming presence, God establishes an intimate relationship between the kingdom and the world. All too often God's people have sought to separate what he has joined together.

One can rightly speak of a biblical this-worldliness which finds its source in the divine creation, the covenant, the incarnation, and the presence of the kingdom. "The earth is the Lord's and the fulness thereof" (Ps. 24:1). The truth about the creation is confessed in the light of God's covenant dealings with humankind. The Word became flesh and dwelt among us. God's covenant was fulfilled in the coming and saving work of Jesus Christ. As Christians we can never again view the world as if the incarnation had never happened, and as if the Holy Spirit is not present in history. On the basis of our covenant-faith, we should no longer view the creation and worldly realities as a fate with which we are burdened. Instead, we must learn to enjoy them in light of the gospel of the kingdom. In Christ all things are ours, including the world (I Cor. 3:22).

Nevertheless, we know that "the form of this world is passing away" (I Cor. 7:31). Our this-worldliness is a *qualified* this-worldliness. It is in faith, hope, and love that we affirm the good earth and the destiny of all things in the kingdom of God. We confess this in spite of the consequences of sin which are seen so clearly around us. We believe that "the world passes away" (I Jn. 2:17), not in total annihilation, but in recreation. The final triumph over sin and death will then be revealed.

There is always the great temptation to turn a qualified this-worldliness into an uncritical world acceptance. The saying, so popular in recent years, that the Church must "let the world set the agenda," contains important insights. As Christians we are often inclined to answer questions that nobody is asking and to be preoccupied with "churchcraft" rather than the desperate needs of the world. On the other hand, such a saying can easily become a mere worldly slogan, and when this occurs, the prophetic witness of the Church loses its critical edge. We become worldly in the wrong way. All sorts of cultural movements become identified with the coming of the kingdom and are seen as new sources of revelation.

It should be pointed out that those who opposed the view that the Church must "let the world set the agenda" were not thereby *ipso facto* protected against the seduction of the spirit of the age. For instance, at the world congress of evangelicals held in Lausanne in 1974, René Padilla of InterVarsity in Argentina warned his fellow-evangelicals against an American "culture-Christianity" which is frequently exported in "evangelical" wrappings. He stressed that a "church growth missiology" which is very much concerned about setting its own agenda can become the expression of a worldly "technological mentality" which is more interested in efficiency than the integrity of the gospel. When that happens, it does not invalidate the insights of a biblical church growth theology; rather it demonstrates the continued effectiveness of the principalities and powers of this world.

By and large, twentieth-century evangelicalism has avoided a kingdom theology out of fear that it would lead to a theological liberalism in which belief in God's transcendent providence is replaced by a belief in this-worldly progress. We have noted already how in nineteenth-century liberalism, with its strong emphasis on human ethical behavior, the kingdom became *moralized* and identified with "progressive" social movements. In reaction against these developments, American evangelicals took refuge in what Martin Marty called a "Private Protestantism" which saw itself in opposition to a "Public Protestantism" which focused on worldly concerns and social witness.

In many evangelical circles, kingdom theology became suspect as a movement that would inevitably thrust the churches into all the alleged evils of the "social gospel." In the process, those evangelicals lost sight of an important aspect of their own heritage, namely the way in which revivalism had often included profound social concern.[10] Furthermore, the "social gospel," particularly as represented in the works of Walter Rauschenbusch, was interpreted one-sidedly from the perspective of nineteenth-century liberalism, ignoring the fact that this movement also drew on elements of the revivalist tradition.

While valid criticisms can be raised against various aspects of Rauschenbusch's theology, he can hardly be accused of having exchanged the biblical message of conversion and future expectation for a totally this-worldly philosophy of human progress. He spoke about the "kingdom ideal" and saw it as "a vital and organizing energy now at work in humanity."[11] But to him this meant that God himself is at work in the world. "It is true," he wrote, "that any regeneration of society can come only through the act of God and the presence of Christ; but God is now acting and Christ is now here."[12] According to Rauschenbusch, Jesus was not a social reformer; "the heart of his heart was religion" and "no man is a follower of Jesus in the full sense who has not through him entered into the same life with God."[13]

The following quote gives one a sense of the flavor and dynamic of Rauschenbusch's kingdom theology:

> It is for us to see the kingdom of God as always coming, always pressing in on the present, always big with possibility, and always inviting immediate action. We walk by faith. Every human life is so placed that it can share with God in the creation of the kingdom or it can resist or retard its progress. The kingdom of God is for each of us the supreme task and the supreme gift of God. By laboring for it we enter into the joy and peace of the kingdom as our divine fatherland and habitation.[14]

Similar ideas can be found in the millennial theology of Alexander Campbell, Charles Finney, and other evangelicals who called for an active or "muscular" Christianity.[15] More than thirty years ago Carl F. H. Henry, in his book *The Uneasy Conscience of Modern Fundamentalism*, tried to persuade evangelicals to pay more attention to the theme of the kingdom of God which, he believed, was central in Jesus' own preaching. Only recently do we see this happening in evangelical circles in the United States and elsewhere. Modern evangelicalism, helped particularly by Christians from the Third World, is rediscovering some of the radical social themes contained in its heritage.

Much of the recent debate on the this-worldly implications of the gospel has been conducted by means of declarations, manifestoes, covenants, and responses that have been issued by various groups. The "Frankfurt Declaration," issued in 1970 by a small group of German university professors and Bible school teachers, was an attack on the World Council of Churches which, the authors believed, had exchanged the true goal of Christian mission for a theory of "humanization" and a "one-sided emphasis on salvation which stresses only this world, according to which the Church and the world together share in a future, purely social, reconciliation of all mankind." We noted earlier that the 1966 Conference on Church and Society and the 1968 Uppsala Assembly had moved the World Council of Churches strongly in the direction of a social action stance. Some of its critics therefore became convinced that social passion had swallowed up soteriological passion.

The "Frankfurt Declaration," which also received wide attention outside of Germany, raised a number of valid concerns that were shared by others within the ecumenical movement, but unfortunately the document was written in such a narrow polemical style and with such "battle language" that its usefulness as a basis for open exchange on the issues was greatly impaired. Nevertheless, a lively discussion on "verticalism" versus "horizontalism" ensued, as participants within the ecumenical movement sought to define their position with respect to the this-worldly implications of the gospel.

While terms like "vertical" and "horizontal" may help to clarify some concerns about various dimensions of the gospel, they soon prove to be wholly inadequate to express the realities of the mystery of the kingdom of God. First of all, "this-versus-that" language usually entails a caricature of viewpoints, since the "vertical" and "horizontal" positions are not to be found in pure form. All parties in the debate hold to a certain dialectic between the world of God's sovereign grace and the world of human social-political responsibilities.

Furthermore, can one—on the basis of the biblical

language itself—ever speak about God in "vertical" terms without stating at the same time that he is Immanuel—God with us? Do we know anything about God independently from his revelation as the One who is "with us?" In short, the mystery of the incarnation and the presence of the kingdom cannot be adequately expressed in our "vertical-horizontal" schemes. If we need to use such language in order to express something about the nature of divine revelation rather than remain silent, we ought to do so with a minimum of dogmatic rigidity.

As a growing number of evangelicals began to express themselves on social issues, the language was no longer exclusively confrontational; a confessional element was introduced into the discussions. In 1973, for example, a group of evangelicals in the United States issued "A Declaration of Evangelical Social Concern," often referred to as the "Chicago Declaration." The document contained the following confession:

> We acknowledge that God requires justice. But we have not proclaimed or demonstrated his justice to an unjust American society. Although the Lord calls us to defend the social and economic rights of the poor and the oppressed, we have mostly remained silent.

The Division of Church and Society of the National Council of Churches, U.S.A., later published a response to the Chicago Declaration which included the following statement:

> While we do not in any way recede from our continuing determination to seek justice for all God's children, we acknowledge that we have not sufficiently shown this determination to be rooted in Christ's gospel.

When combatants start confessing to each other, a whole new climate is usually created. Confession tends to change the ways in which people confront one another. As soon as there is room for self-criticism, a new spirit of openness to receive is bound to follow, which in turn leads to new opportunities for mutual enrichment.

Recent exchanges on the this-worldly implications of the gospel have been conducted not only between evangelicals and ecumenicals, but also between groups within those movements. The Chicago Declaration was basically a message from evangelicals to evangelicals. The Hartford Affirmations, issued in 1975 by a group of eighteen thinkers who belong to various Christian traditions, was basically an appeal from ecumenically oriented Christians to fellow Christians of broad ecumenical persuasion. The signers of the Hartford Affirmations shared a basic concern about the loss of transcendence in much of contemporary church life and thought. The issue was not whether churches should be involved in social issues, but whether, in the name of relevance, basic perspectives of the gospel were being sacrificed, and whether slogans were taking the place of a serious struggling with issues of faith and practice.

The Boston Declaration, published in 1976, came as a reply to Hartford. The opening paragraph states the beliefs and motives that underlie the document:

> The living God is active in current struggles to bring a Reign of Justice, Righteousness, Love and Peace. The Judeo-Christian traditions are pertinent to the dilemmas of our world. All believers are called to preach the good news to the poor, to proclaim release to the captives and recovery of sight to the blind, to set at liberty those who are oppressed and to proclaim the acceptable year of the Lord. Yet we are concerned about what we discern to be present trends in our churches, in religious thought, and in our society. We see struggles in every arena of human life, but in too many parts of the church and theology we find retreat from these struggles. Still, we are not without hope nor warrants for our hope. Hopeful participation in these struggles is at once action in faith, the primary occasion for personal spiritual growth, the development of viable structures for the common life, and the vocation of the people of

God. To sustain such participation, we have searched the past and the present to find the signs of God's future and of ours.

The Boston Declaration concluded with a listing of contemporary movements that can be discerned as signs of "the transforming reality of God's reign today."

A somewhat similar intra-evangelical exchange can be found in the Lausanne Covenant, issued in 1974 by the International Congress on World Evangelization, and "A Response to Lausanne," produced by a minority of participants at that Congress who felt that the official statement did not do justice to the biblical message of radical Christian discipleship. (Modern evangelicalism is increasingly manifesting the kind of diversity that has marked the so-called mainline churches for many years. This is particularly true on issues pertaining to the social implications of the gospel.)

The plethora of documents that have appeared in recent years and the polemics they often embody may obscure the fact that there has been a growing consensus on tbe question of the churches' responsibility toward the world. The burning issue is not so much whether the churches should be concerned about mundane matters, but rather how they should be worldly in the right way and maintain a theological perspective that does justice to all the dimensions of the biblical witness.

The problem has sometimes been that legitimate insights have been turned into slogans and have then become systematized into a "new" theology that dominates the ecclesiastical scene for a season and then fades away. This is what has given some recent theological developments the image of faddism.

Take, for instance, the insight that the proclamation of the gospel itself has had a secularizing influence in the world. An example of this is that the biblical witness to divine creation has radically changed the manner in which people experience and view the world around them. The deification of the forces of nature lies at the heart of much religious mythology. The world is viewed as inhabited and controlled by mysterious and demonic forces. It is not difficult to see why, in that kind of world view, such endeavors as scientific enquiry and technology are not likely to emerge. If one believes that nature is inhabited by god-like powers and is possessed by all kinds of demonic forces, one does not apply research but rather rituals through which one hopes to placate these mysterious and threatening agencies. Through the witness of the Scriptures, people have been taught to look upon nature as divine creation. This is a change in perspective that has immense cultural consequences.

It is true, of course, that the fruits of scientific research and technology have not been unmixed blessings. The demons that have been cast out are often replaced by new and sometimes more destructive ones. The belief in creation, which led to a new openness in the exploration of nature, has frequently become distorted and has then led to exploitation of the world's natural resources. Hendrikus Berkhof has described secularism as "a Christian-anti-Christian phenomenon."[16] Such insights, when incorporated into a theology of the kingdom, are of tremendous significance in shaping the Church's understanding of her mission in the world. However, when turned into slogans, they tend to lead to an uncritical world-acceptance and a loss of prophetic perspective.

The recent discussions on humanization provide another example. What are the implications of the Church's confession that the new humanity has been revealed in Jesus Christ and that he is the first-born of all creation? Does the transforming power of the Holy Spirit, through whom the new creation is present in our midst, have anything to do with the new humanity in Christ? Out of reaction against a dogmatic humanism which leaves little or no room for the transcendent, Christians have often been reluctant to emphasize the idea of *humanitas*. As Alfred Krass has pointed out, a theologian like John Calvin felt very relaxed with the notion and made it a key concept in his own particular brand of political theology.[17]

The Uppsala report on "Renewal in Mission" offered a valid and valuable insight when it stated:

> We belong to a humanity that cries passionately and articulately for a fully human life. Yet the very humanity of man and his societies is threatened by a greater variety of destructive forces than ever. And the acutest moral problems all hinge upon the question: What is man? . . . There is a burning relevance today in describing the mission of God, in which we participate, as the gift of a new creation which is a radical renewal of the old and the invitation to men to grow up into their full humanity in the New Man, Jesus Christ.[18]

All too soon, however, this insight was turned into a slogan. I remember endless meetings in the ecclesiastical bureaucracy during the 1960s, called for the purpose of "goal setting" so that through our "ministries" a fully human community might be established—a community committed to freedom, truth, brotherhood, justice, peace, and personal integrity, as well as the eradication of racism, sexism, militarism, nationalism, and poverty. How glibly we talked about our work on behalf of the victims of dehumanizing power—the poor, the disenfranchised, the oppressed, the alienated! I do not object to the underlying vision, but to the manner in which it was frequently programed, packaged, and removed from the context of the gospel of the kingdom. Only the gospel of the kingdom will save the dream of humanization from an exclusively humanistic bias. Only this gospel will keep the vision alive when the forces of dehumanization prove to be more powerful than had been anticipated.

Finally, a word about the theme of liberation. We are

passing through an era of "Luke 4 theology." The words of
Luke 4:18-19 probably have been among the most quoted
in recent years:

> The Spirit of the Lord is upon me,
> because he has anointed me to preach good news to the
>   poor.
> He has sent me to proclaim release to the captives and
>   recovery of sight to the blind,
> to set at liberty those who are oppressed,
> to proclaim the acceptable year of the Lord.

Profound insights of the Exodus account and the liberating
activities of God in history have been rediscovered, and we
should be deeply grateful for that. Latin American theologians in particular have sought to lead us out of the bondage of abstraction with their insistence that theology and
Christian proclamation grow out of the context of the concrete historical situation.

One day, during the WCC conference on "Salvation
Today" in Bangkok, I walked with the Dutch missiologist
Johannes Verkuyl from an assembly session during which
one of many passionate expositions on Luke 4 had been
presented. I wondered aloud whether we were not in
danger of engaging in theological reductionism by focusing
almost exclusively on that passage. "Yes," Professor Verkuyl replied, "but in my tradition I have heard the ten
commandments recited almost weekly in our worship ser-
vices and I think of the many years during which it never
occurred to me that the Scriptures are speaking about real
liberation in a concrete historical situation. It's time for a
corrective."

In our historical situation, with its growing demand
for freedom and justice by the oppressed peoples of the
earth, the Luke 4 emphasis has indeed provided a necessary
and long overdue corrective. But correctives sometimes
have a way of taking on imperialistic characteristics. This

happens, it seems to me, when the theme of liberation is set *over against* the theme of reconciliation as if the former is more true to the revolutionary nature of the gospel than the latter. It is also important that the basic vision of the gospel not be so closely identified with a certain theological method (for example, Marxist social analysis) that the rejection of certain aspects of the latter blinds one to the validity of the former.

"I do not pray that thou shouldst take them out of the world, but that thou shouldst keep them from the evil one" (Jn. 17:15). Escaping from the world is not an option available to those who seek to be faithful to the gospel. The Church is not called to be an island where God's people huddle together while the traffic of world history passes by. The world and its history are the scene of God's presence, the arena of his struggle with the anti-kingdom forces, and the sphere where the signs of the new world are manifested. We love the world in the name of him who has overcome the world and in the hopeful knowledge that the kingdoms of this world shall become the kingdom of our Lord and of his Christ.

3. KINGDOM AND SELFHOOD

What does all this emphasis on the kingdom and biblical this-worldliness have to say about the cultivation of the inner life? We are pilgrims of the future, not only in the outward sense, but also in the sense of an inward journey. Human beings are historical creatures in a unique way, because in order to be fully human they must constantly be in the process of becoming. Becoming is a dimension of all existence, but the way a person participates or fails to participate in his/her becoming is a uniquely human dimension.

"The longest journey," wrote Dag Hammarskjöld in his book *Markings*, "is the journey inwards."[19] The rest-

less search for self-identity and self-realization is, according to the Scriptures, deeply rooted in the divine creation.
The fact that the human heart hungers for a way that will
lead out of alienation is a sign of the *imago Dei* and the
peculiar spiritual nature of humankind.

We have noted earlier that the gospel of the kingdom
deals with spiritual realities, but that this in no way implies
that reality should be spiritualized. Nor, we must now add,
should spirituality be understood exclusively in terms of
the internal life. All too often the impression has been created
that the more spiritual things are, the more they must be
internalized and individualized. This is certainly not the case
in the Scriptures.

Historically, Christian theology has had much to say
about the *gratia interna* and the *inhabitatio Spiritus
Sancti*. Christ does indeed dwell in our hearts and this
happens through the operation of "his Spirit in the inner
man" (Eph. 2:20). The mystical experience contains an
important dimension of realized or, at least, inaugurated
eschatology. Mysticism and eschatology are, biblically
speaking, intimately related to each other. "It is a tragedy
of Christendom," observed Fison quite correctly, "that
mysticism so easily runs away from eschatology and eschatology so seldom has any use for mysticism." In the
same context he wrote that "a present mysticism to correct
a crude futurist eschatology is as vital as a future eschatology to correct a vague sentimental mysticism."[20]

There have been endless discussions on whether Luke
17:21 declares that the kingdom of God is "within" us or
"in the midst of us." Grammatically, both translations are
possible, and from the perspective of a theology of the
kingdom both express an important truth. The historically
acting God, through the Holy Spirit, is present in history
and dwells in the human heart. A rigid either/or approach
in these matters will inevitably lead to a truncated gospel.

The human search for selfhood is a concern of the

kingdom. The so-called human potential movement, despite its frequent aberrations and absurdities, has helped many people to gain a deeper awareness of themselves. The distortions that usually occur in connection with such movements may lead Christians to dismiss them out of hand rather than enrich them with biblical insights. For instance, the Scriptures make quite clear that the self is not an entity unto itself. Humans were created for community; it is through community that our lives are enriched and made complete. Therefore, a search for selfhood which is nothing but an ego-trip will actually lead to deeper alienation. Martin Buber spoke the prophetic word with his dictum that "all real living is meeting."

Preoccupation with the condition of one's soul without concern about the conditions of society is contrary to the biblical witness. A fascination with selfhood that is combined with an indifference about neighborhood, is clearly a sign of disobedience to the mandate of the gospel. The Copernican revolution in a person's life which the Bible calls conversion becomes manifested in many ways, but especially when a self-centered life becomes Christ-centered and other-oriented. When we die to the self, we become alive to God, and when we become alive to God, we become free for the world of the neighbor. And when we want to know who our neighbors are, the Scriptures point us straight to the needy people in the world. This is a message which our narcissistic era so desperately needs to hear.

"Let no one seek his own good, but the good of his neighbors" (I Cor. 10:24). The Lord taught us to address God as *our* Father and to pray for *our* daily bread. The great Christian mystic Meister Eckhart (1260–1327) wrote the following commentary on that text:

> Bread is given to us not that we eat it alone but that others who are indigent might be participants.... He who does not give to another what belongs to another does not eat his own bread, but another's at the same time with his

own. Thus, when we eat bread acquired justly, we eat our bread; but when bread is acquired by evil means and with sin, we are not eating our own but another's. For nothing that we have unjustly is ours.[21]

The 1970s have been referred to as the "me-decade." Ironically, the me-mentality has been in Christian circles for many years as Christians have sung with great gusto about the grace of God: "Oh, that will be glory for me, glory for me!" The nature of spirituality is one of the most crucial questions facing Christian churches today. It relates to the deepest issues of faith, witness, and life-style. What is needed in our era is a spirituality that will incorporate dimensions of biblical this-worldliness.

Dag Hammarskjöld was one of those rare figures in modern history who was imbued with a mystical-political consciousness. In a script for a radio program, he once wrote:

> the explanation of how man should live a life of active social service in full harmony with himself as a member of the community of the spirit, I found in the writings of those great medieval mystics for whom "self-surrender" had been the way to self-realization, and who in "singleness of mind" and "inwardness" had found strength to say Yes to every demand which the needs of their neighbors made them face. . . .[22]

"Return to the world," said Father Joachim to Nikos Kazantzakis, when the latter went to see him in order to enquire about the holy life. "In this day and age the world is the true monastery; that is where you will become a saint."[23] Sainthood then comes to mean that one has found the spiritual grace to be separated while involved. Jesus too admonished people to be in the world without being of it. He himself is the supreme example of one who was involved in the world in spiritual freedom. Hammarskjöld must have had this kind of sainthood in mind when he wrote, "In our era, the road to holiness necessarily passes through the world of action."[24]

It has been said that in the Christian faith everything begins in mysticism and ends in politics. From the perspective of the gospel of the kingdom that statement contains a substantial element of truth. It should definitely not be interpreted to mean that the kingdom is to be politicized and equated with our causes, platforms and programs. It does mean, however, that the spiritual life always has its political consequences, and, from the perspective of the gospel of the kingdom, we should not wish it to be otherwise. Once we understand this, we are no longer surprised to learn that Meister Eckhart got into trouble with the authorities of his day because of the radical social implications of his preaching, and that Thomas Merton had delivered a speech on "Marxism and Monastic Perspectives" just a few hours before he died.[25] Great Christian mystics have recognized that the spiritual journey is not the same as preoccupation with personal salvation. The Christ who dwells in us is the Christ who died the death of a criminal accused of being a threat to the political order of his day. It is our calling to let him so reign in our hearts that the signs of his lordship become manifested in history.

VI *Christian Mission in Kingdom Context*

1. ESCHATOLOGY AND MISSION

Christian mission takes place in the context of the kingdom of God. In the biblical view of things both the Church and the world must be understood from the perspective of the future of the Lord. It is not the divine intention that the world become the Church, but rather that both the Church and the world find their ultimate destiny in the kingdom. "Church planting," as a dimension of the apostolate, is never an end in itself; it is done to serve the world for the sake of the kingdom. The kingdom sets the agenda; the vision and the values that inspire the Church's ministry find their source in the promise of the new heaven and the new earth.

Faithful mission is a mark of the true Church. According to Jürgen Moltmann, "the *pro-missio* of the kingdom is the ground of the *missio* of love to the world."[1] The God who comes is the Lord of history who calls people into the covenant community and sends them into the world. The apostolate of the Church is not an option; it is the very heartbeat of the Church, its *raison d'être*. The Church discovers its being by engaging in obedient mission.

Christian mission must be seen in light of God's historical-eschatological dealings with the world. Biblical revelation has given the world a true sense of history. "Revelation," writes Moltmann, "recognized as promise and embraced in hope . . . sets an open stage for history, and fills it with missionary enterprise and the responsible exercise of hope, accepting the suffering that is involved in the contradiction of reality and setting out towards the promised future."[2] Revelation, as the redemptive presence of God, makes existence truly historical and imbues the believer with an historical consciousness that becomes expressed in obedient ministry. Christian mission does more, however, than filling the historical interim; it creates history in the power of the Holy Spirit.

The Church's mission takes place in the "last days"—between Pentecost and the Parousia. In the dispensation of the Spirit, God has provided time and space for the Church's apostolate on behalf of the world and for the sake of the kingdom. Mission is done in the authority and the power of the risen Lord. "All authority in heaven and on earth has been given to me. Go therefore and make disciples of all nations" (Mt. 28:18–19). Instead of leading to despair, the "delayed Parousia" led the disciples of Jesus to "the end of the earth" (Acts 1:8).

Periods of intense eschatological expectation have usually been times of strong missionary motivation. When the vision of the future is alive and the expectation of the kingdom is intense, a sense of urgency about mission tends to develop. Johannes Hoekendijk used to say that "the apostolate is impatience in action." It is true that this sense of urgency has sometimes been expressed in a desire to save souls from the imminent doom of eternal perdition, a desire that was often matched by indifference about conditions in society. In other cases, however, the dream of the coming kingdom has provided the motivation and inspiration for a Christian commitment to the righteousness of the kingdom of God which does not compromise the call to personal conversion.

"The future of the kingdom," according to Wolfhart Pannenberg, "releases a dynamic in the present that again and again kindles the vision of man and gives meaning to his fervent quest for the political forms of justice and love."[3] There can be little doubt that it was that kind of dynamic that moved a prophet like Martin Luther King, Jr., in pursuit of his dream. He died a martyr's death, but being dead he still speaks to the minds and hearts of those who hunger and thirst for righteousness:

> I have seen the promised land. I may not get there with you. But it doesn't matter now. We as a people will get to the promised land. My eyes have seen the glory of the coming of the Lord!

The gospel of the kingdom releases a dynamic that has revolutionary potentials. Christian mission is done in the name and the power of him who has declared: "Behold, I make all things new" (Rev. 21:5). It is bound to shake the foundations of self-satisfied lives and *status quo* societies. However, not all revolutionaries are drawn by a vision; there are many revolutionaries who are basically driven by frustration, and it is extremely important that we recognize the difference. The latter frequently will have destructive impulses and, when entrusted with power, are bound to become the purveyors of new tyrannies. There has been an immense amount of romanticizing about revolutions among Christians in recent years.

"Ascetic Christianity," wrote Walter Rauschenbusch, "called the world evil and left it. Humanity is waiting for a revolutionary Christianity which will call the world evil and change it."[4] The tone of that statement seems a bit too triumphalistic and reminiscent of the hymn:

> Rise up, O men of God!
> His kingdom tarries long;
> Bring in the day of brotherhood
> And end the night of wrong.

Yet, a world in need is always waiting for a Christianity that lives and moves and has its full being from a vision

of the future of the Lord, and through its mission seeks to
hasten the day of the coming of the kingdom.

2. PROCLAIMING THE KINGDOM

Jesus was sent for the purpose of preaching the kingdom of
God (Lk. 4:43). The term "preaching" does not exhaust
the nature and meaning of his ministry upon earth, but it
does express something essential about it. We too are sent
to proclaim the gospel of the kingdom of God. While Christian mission encompasses more than preaching, it is hard to
conceive of a dynamic missionary movement that lacks
proclamation.

Through the proclamation of the Word and the power
of the Holy Spirit, the gospel of the kingdom *happens*. The
prophetic witness of the Church is an historical force of the
first order. We are not talking about the efficaciousness of
our talk, but about the power of the living and active Word
of the Lord which is sharper than a two-edged sword (Heb.
4:12). When the Church loses faith in the power of that
Word, an impotence of life and witness soon follows.

Through the proclamation of the Word, God himself
is in our midst and the power of his kingdom is manifested
in history. The gospel of the kingdom, in the power of the
Holy Spirit, creates signs of the future of the Lord upon the
earth. The sermon is not an internal ecclesiastical affair
merely for the spiritual edification of those who attend. It
is that too, but in the context of the kingdom preaching
must first of all be understood as *public* proclamation of the
Word of the Lord to the whole world. The sermon is not a
pep talk; it is a prophetic witness. The name and the will of
God are pronounced upon the earth. Through the Church
"the manifold wisdom of God" is made known to the principalities and the powers (Eph. 3:10). Through the proclamation of the gospel of the kingdom these powers learn the
truth about themselves, namely that the Lord is God and

they are not. Through the proclamation of the Word, the forces of dehumanization in this world are exposed and confronted.

If we focus too much on what happens in our sanctuaries, we tend to become preoccupied with liturgical forms, with the mystery that takes place in the inner sanctum. This is important, but it must be seen in the context of the kingdom, and must be related to culture and to what happens in the streets of the world's towns and cities.

The proclamation of the gospel of the kingdom *has* borne fruit in the cultural life of the nations. It *has* influenced societal structures and legislation. The world is different because prophets of the Lord have spoken and because the seed of the gospel has been sown among the nations. These are not incidental side effects, unrelated to what is supposed to be the real purpose of Christian preaching. It is the real purpose of God that the world be saved from the chaos of sin and that his kingdom be established upon the earth. The prophetic proclamation of the Church is supposed to serve the new order of God. Thus the historically acting God chooses to be actively engaged in the world.

In view of all this, the recent proclamation-versus-presence debates must be considered nothing short of tragic. As if proclamation has nothing to do with presence, and as if Christian presence could ever be severed from the Word and the Spirit and still remain *redemptive* presence! The sad irony of this whole controversy has been that the opposing parties have often helped to bring about these conditions which they confess to fear most.

The advocates of presence fear that Christian witness will be seen exclusively in terms of verbalization, and as a result, the world will be treated to words, words, words, and more words. They are right in insisting that there is more to it than that. For many of these people presence has come to mean social-political involvement. I would certainly not deny that such involvement can indeed be a genuine expression of Christian faith and obedience.

Yet, it must be confessed that advocates of social action often have been more successful in promulgating statement upon statement upon statement than in motivating people to change their way of life. Anyone who has been close to the ecumenical scene knows something about how much energy and time are consumed during statement-writing sessions.

I am well aware that those pronouncements were intended to make a prophetic witness to the world. There are those who deny that they ever did. Jacques Ellul, for instance, writes: "Everyone knows full well that these statements are of no practical use. They are not a way of influencing the government or public opinion. Neither are they Christian witness."[5] This criticism seems overly severe, but surely it is time for the Church to take a long and hard look at its feverish activity of writing prophetic statements (usually composed by committees lodged in comfortable hotel rooms), and to ask itself whether it is in danger of doing the very thing to which it so strenuously objects—producing words, words, and more words.

On the other hand, there are those who believe that preaching is the most important concern in Christian mission. But what does it mean to preach the gospel? Herman Ridderbos has reminded us that when we say that preaching the gospel is *the* task of the Church, we may be saying "more than many people in our churches like to say and like to hear." He goes on to state:

> For the gospel which the Church has to proclaim, is the gospel of the kingdom of God. And if it is true (as I am convinced with all my heart) that the gospel of the kingdom is a message of salvation and liberation of human life, then the Church cannot be silent when she sees men in bondage and slavery (whether spiritual, social, or economical), by their own sins, by the sins of other men, by the political

systems, by the materialistic structure of society, in short
by all the sinful and harmful powers which rule the world
by the grace of Satan and the guilt of men. At stake is the
obedience of the Church to the infallible Word of God. . . .[6]

The problem has often been that those who stress that
the Church must preach Jesus and Jesus alone, have sought
to preach Jesus while remaining silent about justice. This
does not necessarily mean that they have ignored the word
and deed aspects of Christian witness. They have often been
champions of charitable causes. Today, however, people like
Archbishop Dom Helder Camara are reminding us that
"the greatest charity of this century is to help create justice."

How does one preach the Jesus who is revealed to us in
the gospel of the kingdom, who himself made the kingdom
and its righteousness the central focus of his preaching?
Can one forget the issues of justice and still claim to preach
the Jesus of the New Testament? Biblically speaking, justice is hardly a specialized ministry apart from Jesus, nor is
it an optional feature of Christian witness or simply a matter
of individual application of the faith. The Scriptures contain
nothing about an asocial gospel, and the danger of asocial
preaching is that those who express fears about the inroads
of secularism might actually contribute to a spiritual-
cultural vacuum that could eventually be filled by the very
same secular ideologies that they so rigorously denounce.

Finally, a word should be said here about reading the
signs of the times. This is a crucial issue, because the manner in which we read the signs of the times tends to affect
our interpretation of the Scriptures and hence our proclamation of the gospel.

How do we decide whether the kingdom of God is or is
not manifested in particular historical events and
movements? When Harvey Cox, in his book *The Secular
City*, identified certain movements and events in our time
with the breaking in of the kingdom of God, some people
accused him of listing those developments he approved as

signs of the kingdom and those to which he objected as signs of unfaithfulness. Similar questions were raised in connection with the publication of the Boston Declaration, which found "the transforming reality of God's reign" in such temporary movements as the struggle for justice, the drive for ethnic dignity, the women's movement, new models of family relationships, and scientific research.

Some Christians see certain revolutionary movements as the dawn of the new age of the kingdom and its righteousness. Other Christians see the same revolutionary movements as antithetical to the reign of Christ. There are those who condemn all revolutions except, perhaps, the one that brought about the society they wish to preserve.

Reading the signs of the times is risky business. As Jesus pointed out, the difficulty lies not so much in our ignorance, but in our insincerity. "You hypocrites! You know how to interpret the appearance of earth and sky; but why do you not know how to interpret the present time?" (Lk. 12:56). We usually do not do too badly when we study the heavens. However, when we are called upon to interpret history, we tend to be dishonest. The power of self-interest and the need for self-justification frequently take over and distort our perceptions.

We must recognize these dangers. We must search our hearts before we seek to interpret history. Only humble acknowledgement of our own inadequacies and our need for divine guidance and grace will produce a measure of honesty.

Still, there never is assurance that we will read the signs correctly. In short, we must accept a degree of risk. The gospel itself warns us against saying too quickly, "Lo here, or, Lo there!" because the kingdom breaks in at unexpected times (Mt. 24:23 ff.). But venture we must or we shall find ourselves paralyzed by endless analysis and perennial indecisiveness. If we refuse to take a stand on historical events and movements in our day, we end up with a proclamation of the gospel that is not only irrelevant, but unfaithful to our prophetic calling. At heart, Christian witness is an act of faith in the power and grace of a Lord who forgives and continuously sets us free.

3. SERVING THE KINGDOM

Through his Spirit, the ascended Lord sends gifts in order that his people may be equipped for ministry (Eph. 4:12). The Greek word *diakonia* that is used for "ministry" in this instance is also used in the gospels to describe the servant role of Jesus. "For the Son of man also came not to be served but to serve, and to give his life as a ransom for many" (Mk. 10:45). The gospel of the kingdom lays equal stress on the proclamation of the *kerygma* (message) and the practice of *diakonia* (service). Both are grounded in the ministry of Jesus himself, and both take place in the context of the kingdom of God.

The new order of the kingdom, which has been revealed in Jesus Christ, has its own *ethos,* its own rule. "The kings of the gentiles exercise lordship over them; and those in authority over them are called benefactors. But not so with you; rather let the greatest among you become as the youngest, and the leader as one who serves" (Lk. 22:25–26). Here again a derivation of the word *diakonia* is used.

The hymnwriter once more seems to have misunderstood the nature of the gospel when he wrote:

> Rise up, O men of God!
> The Church for you doth wait,
> Her strength unequal to her task;
> Rise up and make her great!

The goal of Christian mission is not the greatness of the Church, but rather the service of the Church to the kingdom.

The very impressive thing about Jesus' ministry was

that he chose to be unimpressive. He emptied himself and assumed the form of a servant (Phil. 2:5 ff.). When tempted by Satan, Jesus refused to follow the road of glamour and self-aggrandizement; he rejected the glory of worldly power. Where he resisted temptation, Christian churches have often succumbed.

There has been much talk in recent years that Christian witness must be expressed in both word and deed. Denominations have developed evangelism programs that use such terms as "Acts Evangelism" (or "Action Evangelism"), "New Life Missioners" and "Evangelistic Life Style." Such emphases have a sound biblical basis. "Let us not love in word or speech but in deed and truth" (I Jn. 3:18). People who do not practice what they preach, who "profess to know God" but "deny him by their deeds" (Ti. 1:16), are an obstacle to true Christian witness. Saying "Lord, Lord" is not enough if one wishes to enter the kingdom of heaven; the will of the Father must be done (Mt. 7:21).

The great American evangelist Charles Finney gave an impressive description of "action evangelism" when he wrote in one of his letters on revivals:

> Now the great business of the Church is to reform the world—to put away every kind of sin. The Church of Christ was originally organized to be a body of reformers. The very profession of Christianity implies the profession and virtually an oath to do all that can be done for the universal reformation of the world. The Christian Church was designed to make aggressive movements in every direction— to lift up her voice and put forth her energies against iniquity in high and low places—to reform individuals, communities, and governments, and never rest until the kingdom and the greatness of the kingdom under the whole heaven shall be given to the people of the saints of the most High God—until every form of iniquity shall be driven from the earth.[7]

The Bible does not advocate a gospel of busyness. Douglas Steere and his fellow Quakers are right when they warn us from time to time against the "heresy of sheer activism." The churches have much to learn from Christian communities like the Quakers about how the call to service and the need for times to "center down" can become integrated into a total Christian life-style. While feverish activism is not the answer to the false quietism that has so often plagued the life of Christian churches, the reemphasis on Christian action in recent years has helped some Christians to rediscover frequently neglected dimensions of the gospel. The biblical emphasis on the poor, the oppressed, and the needy is one of those dimensions. The political dimension of the gospel of the kingdom is another one.

The poor and the needy are usually treated as "problem people," or an unpleasant presence, particularly when they live in the midst of an affluent society. Many people see them only as a burden on the community, and they behave as if most poor people are themselves to be blamed for their poverty. The Bible presents a very different picture, but that view has often not been reflected in the attitudes of church members.

In 1931, the clergy club of New Brunswick, New Jersey, invited the late Professor John Beardslee, a highly respected New Testament scholar at the New Brunswick Theological Seminary, to address them on the subject of "The Kingdom of God." The Clergy Club's program committee was quite explicit in its instructions when it assigned the topic. The speaker was "particularly enjoined to take no notice whatever of any German interpretation and especially warned not in any way to point the bearing of the gospel teachings on the life or problems of the present."[8] It should be pointed out that this statement was made during the Great Depression!

With all due respect for my theological friends in Germany, I am confident that the Church of Jesus Christ will survive such an arbitrary exclusion of their efforts. At least, it would appear to me that the rejection of "any German interpretation" was a less catastrophic decision than the exclusion of "the life or problems of the present" from their considerations of the kingdom of God. What has become of the biblical message about "good news to the poor?"

Paul Minear has observed that "those who were drawn into the kingdom's orbit through Jesus' work comprised a motley company: lepers, harlots, beggars, Pharisees, publicans, soldiers, zealots, fishermen, housewives, the lame, the palsied, the blind."[9] Many of these, no doubt, were "problem people." According to Matthew 25, in the final judgment a basic criterion used to determine who does or does not inherit the kingdom of God will be one's attitudes and actions toward the people who are problems in this world, the ones whom Jesus called "the least of these my brethren."

In the Old Testament "Jubilee legislation" we find not only a concern for poor people, but also a concern about the concentration of wealth in the hands of a few. The matter of the maldistribution of wealth has often been a thorny question for Christians. "Helping the poor" through charitable activities has usually been far more acceptable in church circles than raising questions about economic justice. The scope and impact of Christian charity have indeed been significant. They ought not to be written off in too cavalier a fashion, nor should they be abandoned for a radical rhetoric about systemic change which, all too often, does not become incarnate in a life of service.

One of the more significant developments in our day is the challenge of the economic *status quo* by a number of leading evangelicals who are doing so in the language of faith rather than ideological jargon. Manoel de Mello, founder of the Brazil for Christ Movement, simply talks about "The Gospel with Bread." To him, however, this involves more than charity:

> When I refer to "the Gospel with Bread," I mean to say gospel with health and healing. It is an aspect of bread. The liberation of man is another aspect of bread. Bread is not

limited to a loaf from the bakery for the purpose of eating, rather it is all that which benefits man. Education, to me, is bread. So is clothing. . . . By bread I mean the school, the hospital, just wages, the respect of human personality, the rights of the individual. When I speak of "Gospel with Bread," I am talking about gospel with social justice, with human rights. [10]

But is not such an emphasis in danger of mixing the gospel message with politics? The answer is that the gospel itself has a political dimension. The confession that Jesus is Lord has political implications, as tyrants and dictators have usually noticed. According to the apostle Paul, the political authorities of this world are called to *diakonia*. He refers to those authorities as *"leitourgoi* of God" (Rom. 13:4 ff.). One could speak of a "liturgical service" of the State within the context of the kingdom of God, as long as it is clear that one is talking about a vision of history rather than a simple formula suggesting that a political-action platform can be deduced straight from the Bible. [11]

John Calvin distinguished between the *ministerium* of the Church and the *imperium* of the State. They serve different functions in the context of the kingdom of God. Each is called to a particular *diakonia*. The Church must proclaim the prophetic Word of the Lord. The civil authorities must maintain an order of society which permits a form of *humanitas* to develop in social structures. It has been said that the Church must know the State better than it knows itself. A State that is confronted with the public proclamation of the Word might discover an essential truth about itself, namely its non-divine nature.

Jacques Ellul and others hold that political involvement has usually meant a betrayal of the Church's vocation. [12] It is true that much political involvement of the churches has amounted to an ideological sellout. On the other hand, a non-political gospel has often meant a sellout to secularism in the name of the eternal soul or a worldly cult of success.

Christian *diakonia* takes on many forms. We must avoid both a conservative and a radical type of legalism which presumes to prescribe what is valid Christian witness for everyone in all times and under all circumstances. William Carey (1761–1834), one of the great saints of the evangelical missionary movement, agitated against slavery and organized a boycott against sugar imports from West Indian slave plantations. This does not mean that his action must become a model for every missionary today. But at least it can serve as a reminder that such radical activity in the name of Christian obedience is not an invention of modern-day Marxists.

Diakonia in the context of the kingdom raises critical questions about the life-style of Christians. At heart, the credibility of our message and ministry is at stake. "Take up your cross and follow me," said Jesus. Apparently there is one common denominator in Christian discipleship: it always involves sacrifice.

4. SUFFERING FOR THE KINGDOM

"Jesus," wrote Thomas à Kempis in his *The Imitation of Christ*, "has now many lovers of his heavenly kingdom, but few bearers of his cross." Not much has changed since he wrote that in the 14th century. Costly discipleship is usually more than we Christians bargained for.

The apostle Paul talked in one breath about knowing the power of Christ's resurrection and sharing his sufferings (Phil. 3:10). Sharing in Christ's sufferings means not only that we are prepared to endure persecution for the sake of our faith, but also that we are prepared to share the agonies and sufferings of the spiritually and economically deprived people in the world. Such identification with the needs of others is indeed the most difficult form of Christian witness.

We noted earlier in this study that the Christian faith

is not preoccupied with death. Nietzsche was wrong when he called it a "metaphysics of the hangman." The gospel is not an invitation to failure; it offers victorious living, albeit not triumphalistic living. On the other hand, all blatant attempts to base a cult of success on the message of the crucified Christ ought to be viewed with a good deal of skepticism.

Christ spoke clearly about the price of commitment. "He who loves father or mother more than me is not worthy of me; and he who does not take his cross and follow me is not worthy of me" (Mt. 10:37 f.). "If they persecuted me they will persecute you" (Jn. 15:20). The disciple is not greater than his master.

The early Christians soon discovered the connection between the kingdom and suffering:

> I John, your brother, who share with you in Jesus the trib-ulation and the kingdom and the patient endurance, was on the island called Patmos on account of the word of God and the testimony of Jesus. (Rev. 1:9)

It is not surprising at all that the Greek word *martus* used in the New Testament for "witness" has the same root meaning as the word "martyr." The apostle Paul, in II Thessalonians 1:4-5, writes about the steadfastness and faith of his readers under conditions of persecution, and encourages them with the thought that they are being "made worthy of the kingdom of God for which [they] are suffering."

As participants in and proclaimers of the new order of God, Christians become a threat to the established order. "The 'cross' of Jesus," writes Yoder, "was a political punishment; and when Christians are made to suffer by government it is usually because of the practical import of their faith, and the doubt they cast upon the rulers' claim to be 'Benefactor.'"[13]

It is therefore to be expected that Christians will "be dragged before governors and kings" (Mt. 10:19; see also

Mk. 13:11; Lk. 12:11-12). It is interesting to note that the New Testament sees such persecution as the opportune time for Christian witness to political authorities. Krister Stendahl has pointed out that "the Christian before the courts is the only one to whom the Scriptures promise the gift of the Spirit."[14] The Spirit will provide the "tongue" for those who are called to testify before the authorities.

Proclamation of the kingdom implies protest against much that has become sacred in the established order. This was true for Dietrich Bonhoeffer and others during the Nazi era, and it is true today in every country of the world where the gospel of the kingdom is being proclaimed.

Years ago Walter Rauschenbusch voiced the following opinion: "The championship of social justice is almost the only way left open to a Christian nowadays to gain the crown of martyrdom. Theological heresies are rarely persecuted now."[15] As we look around the world today, we see substantial evidence of the truth of this statement. Numerous Christians are suffering for the sake of the kingdom because they advocate justice. True, there are other forms of discrimination against those who because of their Christian conviction refuse to conform to the predominant cultural values and practices. But most of those who are dying for their Christian witness today are people who, in the words of the apocalypse cited earlier, are sharing "in Jesus the tribulation and the kingdom," and who are doing so as advocates of justice.

By saying this, we are once again treading on dangerous ground. Just because prophets usually get into trouble, that does not mean that everyone who is in trouble is in that situation because of a prophetic stance. Pastors in particular are sometimes all too eager to blame their difficulties on the stand they have taken for righteousness and truth, when in so many cases their insensitivity and ideological dogmatism have contributed substantially to their tribulations and tensions.

Yet, we should have no illusions about the realities of Christian social witness. For instance, when Carl F. H. Henry calls for "a cadre of concerned persons willing to be publicly identified in active, vocal confrontation"[16] for the sake of social justice, he is calling people to what will most likely prove to be a costly discipleship. After all, very little has changed since those behind the commercial interests of Ephesus (Acts 19) went after Paul and his associates, claiming that preaching the gospel was bad for business.

5. PRAYING FOR THE KINGDOM

"Thy kingdom come!" This is a revolutionary prayer. It expresses the passionate longing for a new order of things. When we pray "Thy kingdom come," we say in effect: "O Lord, hasten the day when our 'orders,' which are in so many cases institutionalized selfishness and programed injustice, will make way for the new order of your kingdom."

The Talmud teaches, "That prayer in which there is no mention of the kingdom of God is not a prayer." We have so many needs and petitions to be brought before the throne of grace. But, according to the biblical vision, the kingdom is God's ultimate answer to the world's needs. The prayer "Thy kingdom come" issues from a dual knowledge: the knowledge that God's kingdom has indeed come, and the knowledge that all our accomplishments, no matter how impressive they may seem, will not bring about its consummation. We pray for the kingdom because we have experienced the power of the new age. On the other hand, in our encounter with the living Lord, we become more deeply aware of the limitations of our own power.

Yet, prayer is not an act of total resignation. We pray as those who are in a covenant relationship with God—a covenant partnership. Therefore, prayer must never become a substitute for obedience and responsible action. Hence the hastening on to the words, "Thy will be done on earth as it is in heaven." The divine initiative comes first. But in the covenant relationship our response, by God's grace, becomes an integral part of the divine action.

Prayer itself can be a political and even revolutionary act. In some oppressive situations it is the only kind of service on behalf of the world that is left to Christians. Jacques Ellul, referring to worldly rulers, states:

> it is precisely the demonic character of the power which makes prayer the most important political action that the Christian could possibly take, prayer which is a sharing in the struggle of Jesus, prayer that the authorities might be brought into subjection, prayer that they might be exorcised, prayer that their power might be turned toward justice and good. Prayer is much more important than all the declarations, demonstrations, elections, etc.[17]

Intercession for those who are in positions of authority and power is one of the most important ministries of the Church. It too finds its meaning in the context of the kingdom of God.

Prayer for the coming of the kingdom issues from the joyful knowledge that the Lord is faithful. He, who is "able to do far more abundantly than all that we ask or think" (Eph. 3:20), will do what he has promised.

> Thy kingdom come...
> For thine is the kingdom, and the
> power, and the glory. Amen.

Notes

CHAPTER I

1. See Ralph G. Wilburn, *The Historical Shape of Faith* (Philadelphia, 1966), pp. 22 f.
2. John Bright, *The Kingdom of God* (New York, 1953), pp. 9 ff.

CHAPTER II

1. *Institutes of the Christian Religion*, I, viii, 1.
2. Georgia Harkness, *Understanding the Kingdom of God* (Nashville, 1974), p. 92.
3. Herman Ridderbos, *The Coming of the Kingdom* (Philadelphia, 1962), pp. 121 f.
4. See his *Commentary* on Luke 11:2.
5. Jim Wallis, *Agenda for Biblical People* (New York, 1976), p. 23.
6. See his *The Kingdom of God in America* (New York, 1937), p. 141.
7. *Gospel in Context*, Vol. I, No. 3, July 1978, p. 20.
8. *Ibid.*, p. 23.
9. *Theology of the New Testament*, I (New York, 1951), p. 335.

CHAPTER III

1. *The Prophetic Faith* (New York, 1960), p. 28.
2. Jacques Ellul, *False Presence of the Kingdom* (New York, 1972), p. 178.
3. Cf. Paul Schütz, cited in Jürgen Moltmann, *Theology of Hope* (New York, 1967), p. 227.
4. See Richard John Neuhaus in Wolfhart Pannenberg, *Theology and the Kingdom of God* (Philadelphia, 1969), p. 25.

5. George S. Hendry, *The Gospel of the Incarnation* (Philadelphia, 1958), p. 48.

6. Jean Daniélou, *The Lord of History* (London, 1958), p. 2.

7. See his *Christ, the Christian and the Church* (London, 1946), p. 69.

8. *Ibid.*, p. 150.

9. *Ibid.*, p. 76.

10. Paul S. Minear, *The Kingdom and the Power* (Philadelphia, 1950), p. 224.

11. Cf. his *The Politics of Jesus* (Grand Rapids, 1972), p. 61.

12. Herman Ridderbos, *Paul* (Grand Rapids, 1975), pp. 48, 54.

13. Cf. T. F. Torrance, *Kingdom and Church* (Edinburgh, 1956), p. 162.

14. *Op. cit.*, p. 132.

CHAPTER IV

1. Jürgen Moltmann, *The Church in the Power of the Spirit* (London, 1977), p. 192.

2. Jacques Ellul, *False Presence of the Kingdom* (New York, 1972), p. 24.

3. T. F. Torrance, *Kingdom and Church* (Edinburgh, 1956), p. 5.

4. Roger L. Shinn, *Christianity and the Problems of History* (New York, 1953), p. 32.

5. Donald Sneen, *Visions of Hope* (Minneapolis, 1978), p. 127.

6. *Sojourners*, October, 1978, p. 36.

7. See his "Politics and the Practice of Hope," *Christian Century*, 11 March 1970, pp. 288–291.

8. Cf. *The Secular City Debate*, ed. Daniel Callahan (New York, 1966), pp. 129–156.

9. Exchanges on this subject can be found in some of the 1977 issues of *The Reformed Journal* and *Sojourners*.

10. Cited in I. C. Rottenberg, *Redemption and Historical Reality* (Philadelphia, 1964), p. 17.

11. H. Berkhof, *Christ the Meaning of History* (Richmond, 1966), p. 175.

12. *Ibid.*, p. 122.

13. *Op. cit.*, p. 39.

14. H. R. Niebuhr, *The Kingdom of God in America* (New York, 1937), p. 193.

15. Alfred C. Krass, *Five Lanterns at Sundown* (Grand Rapids, 1978), p. 61.

16. Jacques Ellul, *op. cit.*, pp. 20 f.

17. *Op. cit.*, p. 191.

CHAPTER V

1. J. E. Fison, *The Christian Hope* (London, 1954), p. 40.
2. *Ibid.*, p. 41.
3. Cf. I. C. Rottenberg, *Redemption and Historical Reality* (Philadelphia, 1964), pp. 52 f.
4. See his *On the Philosophy of History* (New York, 1957), p. 150.
5. *The Documents of Vatican II* (New York, 1966), p. 79.
6. Cited in I. C. Rottenberg, *op. cit.*, p. 123.
7. See the article "An Eastern Orthodox Viewpoint," by George Khodr, interviewed by Paul Löffler in *International Review of Mission*, Vol. LX, No. 237, January, 1971, p. 68.
8. Jürgen Moltmann, *The Church in the Power of the Spirit* (London, 1977), p. 235.
9. *Ibid.*, p. 251.
10. On this topic Donald W. Dayton's book *Discovering an Evangelical Heritage* (New York, 1976) is a rich source of information.
11. Walter Rauschenbusch, *A Theology for the Social Gospel* (Abingdon Paperback, Nashville, 1945), p. 165.
12. Walter Rauschenbusch, *Christianity and the Social Crisis* (New York, 1907), p. 346.
13. *Ibid.*, pp. 47 f.
14. *A Theology for the Social Gospel*, p. 141.
15. Cf. H. R. Niebuhr, *The Kingdom of God in America* (New York, 1937), pp. 154 f.
16. H. Berkhof, *Christ the Meaning of History* (Richmond, 1966), pp. 91–98.
17. Alfred C. Krass, *Five Lanterns at Sundown* (Grand Rapids, 1978), pp. 134 f.
18. *The Uppsala Report*, 1968, p. 27.
19. *Markings* (New York, 1964), p. 58.
20. *Op. cit.*, p. 186.
21. Matthew Fox, "Meister Eckhart and Karl Marx: The Mystic as Political Theologian," *Listening* (Journal of Religion and Culture), Vol. 13, No. 3, Fall 1978, p. 235.
22. *Op. cit.*, p. VII.
23. Nikos Kazantzakis, *Report to Greco* (New York, 1965), p. 305.
24. *Ibid.*, p. 122.
25. Cf. Matthew Fox, *op. cit.*, p. 233.

CHAPTER VI

1. Jürgen Moltmann, *Theology of Hope* (New York, 1967), p. 224.
2. *Ibid.*, p. 86.

3. *Theology and the Kingdom of God* (Philadelphia, 1969), p. 80.

4. *Christianity and the Social Crisis* (New York, 1907), p. 91.

5. Cf. *False Presence of the Kingdom* (New York, 1972), p. 92.

6. "Church, World, Kingdom," a lecture delivered at the Second International Conference of Institutions for Christian Higher Education, held in Grand Rapids, Michigan, August 13–19, 1978.

7. Cf. Donald W. Dayton, *Discovering an Evangelical Heritage* (New York, 1976), p. 21.

8. John W. Beardslee, Jr., "The Kingdom of God," *The New Brunswick Seminary Bulletin*, Vol. VII, No. 1, March 1932, p. 5.

9. Paul S. Minear, *The Kingdom and the Power* (Philadelphia, 1950), p. 62.

10. Cf. *Monthly Letter about Evangelism* issued by Commission on World Mission and Evangelism, World Council of Churches (Geneva), July 1974.

11. Richard Mouw's use of the term "political evangelism" in his book by that title as well as in his more recent *Politics and the Biblical Drama* (1976), expresses a concern to see political action as an aspect of the evangelistic task of the Church which is as central to the Christian's calling as "personal evangelism." This is an important point. At the same time, however, it should be kept in mind that "personal evangelism," even when it seeks to preach a non-political gospel, has often produced significant, albeit perhaps unexpected, cultural and political fruits. For instance, personal evangelism is frequently accompanied by Bible distribution and in the long run the Scriptures have a way of doing their own radical thing. The sad truth is that the churches are then often the ones that are taken by surprise!

12. *Op. cit.*, pp. 120 ff.

13. John Howard Yoder, *The Politics of Jesus* (Grand Rapids, 1972), p. 128.

14. Krister Stendahl, *Paul among Jews and Gentiles* (Philadelphia, 1976), p. 120.

15. *Op. cit.*, p. 418.

16. Cf. Robert A. Coughenour's review article of Henry's *A Plea for Evangelical Demonstration* in the *Reformed Review* (Vol. 28, No. 1, Autumn 1974), p. 15.

17. *Op. cit.*, p. 112.